CMC offers seminars
that expand and compliment
the "Achieving Profit Potential" Series.

Thanks again for the outstanding seminar! I have always been skeptical when it comes to consultants, but you have really enlightened my thinking, and motivated me to not only make EIS a great company, but to also realize the untapped potential within me! I look forward to our next meeting.

Mike Cody, Sales Manager
Eaheart Industrial Service, Richmond VA

The seminar I attended last Thursday and Friday was by far the best I have attended in my almost 30 years in the business. I learned more in two days than I thought possible.

Gene Medeiros, Product Support Manager
Reliable Tractor Inc, Tifton, GA

I am currently on my flight to Vancouver and I felt it was important that I communicate my extreme satisfaction on attending your *Service Department: Achieving Profits* seminar over the last two days.

As I review the seminar content I am finding myself able to validate many things you are doing well as a service company and equipment dealer. I have also found many great tools to help make us far more profitable and help us retain and attract more top level employees.

The original investment in this seminar will be paid for 10 fold within the first day as I increase our labour rates and implement a service truck charge to recover our costs associated for this expense.

Again, thanks for your personal time, incredible insight and validation that you are on the correct path in our aftermarket business.

Chuck Dietrich, General Manager, Service
Leavitt Machinery, Coquitlam, BC

CURRIE
MANAGEMENT
CONSULTANTS

FLEET

MANAGEMENT

WORKBOOK

ACHIEVING

PROFIT POTENTIAL

IN THE NEW MILLENNIUM

Currie Management Consultants, LLP

67 Millbrook St, Suite 504
Worcester, MA 01606

Telephone: 508-752-9229
Fax: 508-752-9226
E-Mail:cmc@CurrieManagement.com

Currie Management Consultants, LLP
67 Millbrook Street, Suite 504
Worcester, MA 01606
USA

Book design and production by George M. Keen

This book has been written by the Currie Management Consultants, LLP staff. Robert P. Currie, senior partner; Michelle B. Currie, managing partner; George M. Keen, partner; Matthew J. Hicks, associate consultant; Jeffrey R. LaBonte, associate consultant. Additional contributions were from previous employees and associates.

Web site: www.CurrieManagement.com

ISBN : 0-9724917-8-3

Currie Management Consultants, LLP **Profit Potential Series** is available at special discounts for bulk purchase by corporations, institution, and other organizations. For more information, please contact Seminars@CurrieManagement.com, Currie Management Consultants, LLP at the above address or **Wandering Brothers Publishing** at Publishing@wanderingbrothers.com

Wandering Brothers Publishing, CO

Table of Contents

Table of Figures

Overview

Over the thirty plus years of my business experience, there has been a dramatic increase in business publications—books, articles, papers, tapes, and web casts. Previously, you read Drucker, Argyris, and Sloan, subscribed to HBR, Fortune and Business Week, and followed the careers of leaders like Jack Welch.

Today you are bombarded with "business improvement" concepts and ideas. Some of it is "quick fix", and some are real strategic, renewal actions. As valuable as these ideas are, they must be implemented at the right time, capitalizing on opportunities, and achieving breakthrough processes for improved sales and profits.

> **O**pportunity is rooted in customers' desire for more efficiency and effectiveness in their own organizations

For distribution organizations, you believe a dramatic opportunity has presented itself around which you should tailor our organizations. That opportunity is rooted in customers' desire for more efficiency and effectiveness in their own organizations. That opportunity is called outsourcing, Fleet Management, one stop shopping, partnering and other such designations as the latest business writer might invent. Basically, a rapidly increasing number of customers today want more than quality products. Quality and competitive prices are givens—look at how Nissan and Toyota have transformed (captured?) the US auto market.

On the industrial side, feature content, reliability, price and financing are all important sales items, but collectively, they are not the critical value proposition in 21st century marketing.

Beyond product and price, the customer wants service. Service starts with mechanical repair service, but today extends to factors beyond repair. Basically, these extended factors center on ease of ownership. You are moving from marketing a product-centered value proposition, to marketing a "cost of ownership" value proposition, and ultimately to an "ease of ownership" one. Customers want quality products and world class service, but they don't want to think about it. They want you to help manage their businesses by managing the totality of the products and services you provide. (Yes, some day they will want you to also provide the operator.)

No other entity is more correctly poised to capitalize on this change, from product centered to service centered, than distribution Thus, this outsourcing, Fleet Management, one-stop-shopping process is today's battleground for long term strategic domination of a market, and for short and medium term relationships with clients. (Long term relationships will depend on your ability to anticipate and execute the next change.)

No other entity is more correctly poised to capitalize on this change, from product-centered to service-centered, than distribution. Today's distribution has the opportunity to move the customer from traditional "product-brand" relationship to a "service" relationship. Thus, dealer branding (service branding) is or will replace manufacturing branding.

Today's manufacturers that have a firm, integrated, fully developed strategic alliance with distribution will also capitalize on this market change as they transform their distribution into a service-rich organization. Those manufacturers that don't have this vision will be pressured constantly to improve the distribution transaction (features and prices) and will not participate in the full "seed-to-flower" customer relationship and revenue stream. Sometimes these manufacturers that don't share the service-rich vision seek alternative channels to market, which generally reinforces the transaction-rich and not service-rich approach.

This book is intended to help distribution and the manufacturers they represent to understand and begin implementing the process of one-source relationships. Remember, the advantage of one-source relationships to distributors is that all such relationships are viewed by customers as value-based, unique and integrated into their business performance. Therefore, you present this process, this series of steps, to guide you through designing a unique, value-based, service-rich solution for each customer. It is not a "cookie cutter" approach. Outsourcing requires your organization to be skilled at examining data and designing unique solutions. It requires management that fosters employee development, organizational creativity, and autonomous actions.

This is the future of distribution ... and ... it is richly profitable and eminently sustainable.

Robert P. Currie
Senior Partner

Introduction

Purpose of the
Fleet Management Book

This book has been developed for dealers and distributors solely for their use in pricing, selling, implementing, and monitoring Equipment Fleet Management business. It contains guidelines for developing Fleet Management accounts from a strategic point of view and operational tools for implementing the strategy.

While all conditions for Fleet Management can not be anticipated, you have done an extensive investigation of dealers and manufacturer's experience with Fleet Management, Long Term Rentals, and Guaranteed Maintenance contracts. You have endeavored to include charts, spreadsheets, discussion points and ideas in many areas that will help you in developing your program. The guidelines presented here should be viewed not as absolute policy, but as reference for conducting a profitable Fleet Management business. As Fleet Management contracts increase throughout the dealer network, data will increase and the process will evolve.

Definition of Fleet Management

Fleet Management is the total management of a user's fleet of equipment. For a fixed term, the customer completely outsources their equipment management. The dealership:

- Identifies the needs of the customer
- Provides equipment
- Maintains the equipment
- Administers the entire process

In some cases, the dealership may even provide operators for the equipment. The scope of the agreement will vary depending on the needs of the customer, the capabilities of the dealership, and the profitability of each product segment. The key element of this service is that the dealership owns the equipment and is managing the equipment process, rather than the customer.

Benefits of Fleet Management

Fleet Management benefits the dealership, the manufacturer, and the customer.

Benefits to the Dealership

The dealership captures the full business opportunity from the account. Revenue is increased, due to supplying all unit, service, and parts needs. Gross profit as a percent of that revenue increases, because the dealer shifts the product mix to primarily their own brand units and parts.

The marketshare of the dealership increases if the Fleet Management account was not supplied entirely by the dealership before the contract was signed.

Customer satisfaction and retention is increased as the dealership has regular reviews with the account and ample opportunity to maintain a positive relationship.

Cash flow is stabilized because the dealership receives regular monthly payments from the account and can plan for its own expenses related to maintenance of the fleet more easily.

Finally, the dealership benefits from the ability to source rental and used equipment from and to these Fleet Management accounts.

Benefits to the Manufacturer

The benefits to the dealer network in terms of increased profitability and account stability strengthen the entire manufacturer's distribution process.

Supporting customers in all phases of their equipment process evolution increases customer satisfaction, and thus increases customer loyalty to the network.

As the manufacturer's dealers manage the shift of account product mix and parts sourcing, the manufacturer's marketshare and profitability increase.

Benefits to the Customer

There is an expense savings to the account for outsourcing the Fleet Management process. Both direct costs and administrative and accounting expenses are analyzed, and the Fleet Management contract is written to assure savings to the account.

The customer enjoys increased financial stability. First, the account receives a cash increase due to the sales of equipment and parts to the dealership. Second, the fixed assets, equipment and parts, of the customer are decreased on the balance sheet. The increase in cash may allow the account to expand, diversify or reinvest in the account's core business. The shift from fixed assets to current assets will increase the current ratio of the account and allow the company to better meet its current financial obligations. In whatever way the company decides to use the cash, it will be a benefit to the customer.

The change in Fleet Management will increase the uptime of the customer's fleet. Presumably the dealership will manage the maintenance schedules of the units and their replacement cycles at the optimum level, thus maximizing performance of the fleet. In addition, the dealership will have determined the optimum number of units to have in the fleet and will have backup equipment available at all times.

Finally, Fleet Management enables the account to focus on their core business. By invoicing the customer on a set schedule and only for the Fleet Management contract, there are savings in accounting and administrative time. In addition, customers do not need to track their costs or utilization per unit, and need no buying process or personnel for the fleet. The dealership performs these services and reports the information to the account in a summarized fashion. The benefit to the customer of shifting this responsibility is a reduction in the requirement for skilled management employees, which will enable the company to utilize its managers in different areas.

The Fleet Management Process

The process of obtaining Fleet Management contracts and implementing them in a profitable manner contains seven steps in three sections (Preparing for Action – Chapter 1; Sales Action Plan – Chapters 2-5 and then Performing to Contract – Chapters 6-7). The chapters of this book directly mirror those steps. The process chart following this section outlines the steps and can be used as reference. Note the three consensus points contained in the Sales Action Plan. You must continually be confirming your estimates and assumptions with the client to ensure the progress of the deal.

Preparing for Action

1. Identifying & Profiling Target Accounts

The first step in obtaining accounts is to identify the appropriate accounts to target. Here you will find information on gathering account data, segmenting your accounts, prioritizing those accounts, and identifying the accounts most likely to be receptive to, and benefit from Fleet Management.

Sales Action Plan

Once the target accounts have been identified, the sale must be executed. There are four steps in the Sales Action Plan.

2. Approach Account

In this chapter four entry strategies are outlined. Depending on the dealership capabilities and the level of interest the customer has in Fleet Management, you must choose the entry strategy most appropriate, and execute it. If the customer then shows interest in Fleet Management, you will proceed to step 3, Perform Customer Analysis. If not, a new entry strategy should be chosen and executed.

3. Perform Customer Analysis

When a target account expresses interest, an analysis must be done of the equipment needs of the account and their current cost situation. Here you will find information and tools related to gathering application data, current acquisition cost data, current usage cost data, and current administrative cost data.

You'll also gather the customer's business projections and industry data. Analyzing and summarizing that data is covered, along with formatting and presenting it to the customer account.

The key to moving ahead in the process is to then gain consensus on the account's current total cost. If consensus is reached, you can go ahead and estimate your cost of managing the same fleet. If the customer does not agree with your current cost analysis, you must review your data with the customer and revise it as necessary.

4. Developing Pricing

When a consensus has been reached as to the account's current costs, the dealership must then develop its own pricing to provide Fleet Management to the account. First, you must determine the appropriate fleet to service the account. Then you must estimate the acquisition, usage, and administrative costs of providing that fleet at the financial model level. Finally, you must develop your profit expectation for the account based on a comparison of current cost and your pricing, and specific characteristics of the account. All of these issues are covered in this chapter and the methodology of developing pricing yourself.

5. Structure Proposal

Based on your calculated cost compared to the current customer's cost, you must first determine the scope of the program you plan to propose. Next you must outline the program, how it will be implemented, and how the economics of the program will unfold. The entire proposal must be summarized in the executive summary and must be presented to the account. If the proposal is accepted, the contract must be written and then implemented in a profitable manner. If it is not accepted, you must review the proposal process and adjust it accordingly.

This section outlines the elements that must be included in the proposal.

Performing to Contract

In order to execute the contract profitably, there are initial actions to take, and then ongoing processes to follow.

6. Initial Actions

Immediately after the contract comes into effect, several actions must be taken. The fleet must be purchased by the dealership and re-rented back to the account. Any addition to staffing that the dealership needs to execute the contract must be completed. All dealership employees who will be working on the contract or involved with the reporting or billing must be trained in the processes they must follow. All equipment must be serviced, and all operators trained. The processes to follow to perform these initial functions are covered in this chapter of the book.

7. Ongoing Functions

Processes must be developed and followed concerning the equipment replacement cycle, service of the fleet, rental units to support the fleet, and the administration of the contract. Operating, tracking and reporting guidelines are given in this section to enable the performing and monitoring of the contract.

Fleet Management Process

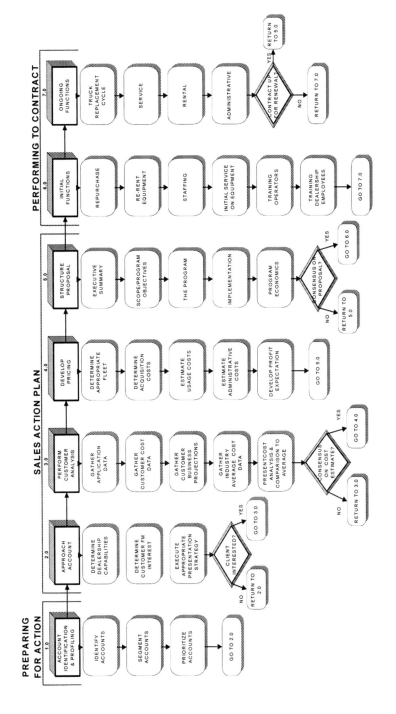

Table 1 Fleet Management Process

1. Identifying and Profiling Target Accounts - (Preparing for Action)

Overview

This section will describe the first step in the process of implementing a Fleet Management program: deciding which accounts to target. You will walk through the steps of identifying ac-counts, segmenting the account database and prioritizing the accounts. This process will enable the dealership to see which accounts are most likely to be receptive to Fleet Management, and therefore warrant utilizing resources for targeting these accounts.

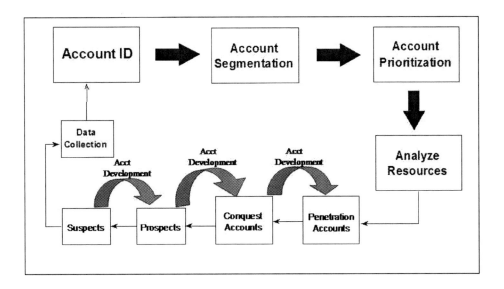

Table 2 : The Sales Management Process

You want to be sure you are aware of all of the equipment users in our territory, so you first discuss ways to identify all of these customers and enter them into a useful database. The next step is to segment this database in a meaningful way. This segmentation is performed along several dimensions based on the customer's potential, interest in Fleet Management and the level of benefit they would gain from the program. Finally, the dealer must take these "target" accounts and determine which ones should be approached based on the dealer's strategic priorities and available resources. This is the prioritization phase.

Each of the boxes in the chart represents a stage in the process described. The boxes in the bottom of the diagram represent the four categories of accounts that you will have our salespeople calling on. Penetration ac-

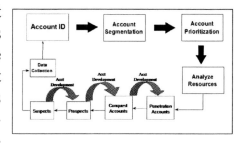

counts are those with which you are currently doing some business but represent an opportunity for increased sales. These will be our initial Fleet Management targets. Conquest accounts are companies that regularly purchase equipment, parts, and maintenance, but from a competitive line. Prospect accounts are companies that fall within a segment you have decided to target (a specific SIC[1] code for instance). You have information about the account but have not been in regular contact with them. Suspects are those accounts that exist, but you know little or nothing about.

Referring again to the Sales Management Process Chart, the goal should be to move the accounts through the stages; suspects should become prospects, then conquest accounts, then

---

[1] SIC refers to the "Standard Industry Code" used in USA business references. The concept is to organize industries of similar type.

penetration accounts. As you collect information on these accounts, you repeatedly proceed through the steps of identifying suspects, segmenting the accounts, prioritizing the accounts, and determining our resource availability in order to decide which entry strategy is most appropriate (this will be discussed further in Chapter 2). It may be helpful to refer to this diagram as you read through this chapter.

Account Identification

In the account identification stage, you should try to identify all of the equipment end users in our territory. This should be a thorough investigation to determine if there are any accounts that you do not know about, and you should be trying to gather comprehensive data about these companies. Next, you will look at each of the steps in this process in more detail.

As with any sales program, the first step is to identify those accounts you wish to target. A comprehensive sales strategy begins with a listing of all of the potential users of equipment in each dealer's area. Where can you begin gathering this data?

Customer Database

Each dealership should have some sort of database they use to track accounts whether they are existing or potential customers. The installed equipment database should include:

- Unit Number/Serial Number
- Who Owns the Unit
- Year Sold
- Model
- Who Services the Unit
- Contact Person
- Replacement Cycle Time

In addition, for all accounts – existing and prospective – you should have a profile containing the following information:

- Company Name
- Address
- City, State, ZIP Code, Phone
- Account Number
- Number of Installed Units
- Account Category (A,B,C,D)
- SIC Code
- Key Contacts
- Special Comments
- Mailing address (if different)

Information Services

Services such as Lexis-Nexis or Dun and Bradstreet specialize in providing customized lists for businesses. You can provide the service with certain criteria (annual revenue, number of employees, location by ZIP code, etc.) and receive, for a fee, a list of businesses meeting these criteria. This option can get expensive but is typically quite complete.

Your Own Research

You generally have plenty of information about our existing customers. What you often lack is detail about potential customers such as: number of employees, annual revenue, types of equipment they have, age of their equipment, etc. Salespeople should be required to gather and enter such data into some type of database following each sales call. You may also want to consider taking on a college intern who could peruse the various sources of industry information found in most public libraries. The more information you can gather on potential and competitive accounts, the easier your job will be.

There are a variety of ways to identify all of the accounts in our territory and to get certain information on them. The sales force can then call on these accounts, gather additional information, and enter it into a database. Once you have this starting point, you can begin the process of segmenting, prioritizing, and targeting selected accounts.

Segmenting Accounts

The purpose of segmenting accounts is to identify the group of accounts to which a sales effort will most likely end in a Fleet Management contract that is beneficial to both the customer and to the dealer. To that end, you want to identify accounts that are in a Phase IV buying mode in terms of market evolution (to be described in this chapter). You can assume that these accounts will be most interested in a Fleet Management program for the following reasons:

- They are large enough accounts to benefit from total outsourcing and to make our sales effort worth-while.
- They spend a significant amount of money on equipment which should make them particularly interested in total process savings.

You walk through segmenting along three dimensions: size of the account, the account's phase of market evolution, the account's consumption of equipment and services.

Segmenting by Size

The first and easiest way to segment your account database is by size. These will be referred to as "A", "B", "C" and "D" accounts. The breakdown is given in the following table, along with the typical percentages of accounts that fall into each category and the revenue they account for.

Category[2]	% of Accounts	% of Sales
"A" = 26+ Units	3%	40%
"B" = 11-25	12%	30%
"C" = 4-10	25%	20%
"D" = 1-3	60%	10%

Table 2: Account Categories Based on Fleet Size

Large accounts will tend to realize the most benefit from Fleet Management since their fleets are large enough to consume a significant portion of the company's operating budget. Larger accounts will usually be more sophisticated in terms of financial management and information systems allowing them to provide us with the cost data you will need to develop a Fleet Management proposal and to understand the significance of the various cost areas. However, size can not be the only factor that you use to target accounts as will discussed in the following sections.

In order to determine fleet size, the best approach is to physically count the units. If this is not possible due to lack of contact with the account, multiple locations etc., you can either rely on information provided by the account or estimate the fleet size using the Consumption Matrix that is introduced later in this section.

---

[2] While this unit segmentation works in many industries, it will not work in all industries. But where equipment is dominant, you will be surprised at how closely this will follow.

Segmenting By Buying Phase

Businesses within an industry will evolve through four phases of market evolution. These phases are defined by how customers make their buying decision. As companies become more and more sophisticated – moving towards Phase IV – they begin to focus more on the cost of the Fleet Management process as opposed to the product alone. The following diagram illustrates this evolution.

Evolution of the Market

	Phase I	Phase II	Phase III	Phase IV
Innovation	Quality	Cost Reduction	Asset Management	Risk Relief
Marketing View of the World	Premium Product ↓ Premium Price	Premium Product ↓ Low Price	Premium Product ↓ Low Cost of Ownership	Premium Process ↓ Low Cost of Process
Customer Focus	Product	Price	Ownership Cost	Outsourcing
Sales Differentiation	Best Product Available	Lowest Cost Provider	Total Cost of Ownership	One Source
Organization Structure	Unit Sales	Rent to Sell & Aftermarket	Lease with Maintenance	Rent to Rent Outsourcing

Table 3 : The Evolution of the Market

Phase I

The account is concerned with innovation in its equipment process through an innovation in the product. That innovation

---

comes about because of either a change in the or a change in the industry. The account might suddenly be large enough to use equipment for the first time, or to use a certain type to do the job in a new way. On the other hand, a new model might have come out, offering a new process option to the account. An alternative might include an account that simply wasn't aware of a process option until your dealership described it.

Phase II

The account is still product oriented, concerned with improving the existing process by way of reducing product price.

Phase III

The account is concerned with improving the existing process through the product, but is now examining the entire cost of ownership of the product. The analysis will have involved the cost of maintaining the equipment and its estimated useful life. The process may have been to determine the appropriate time to replace a unit or to design a rental or lease with maintenance program to minimize total cost for the account.

Phase IV

At this point, the account is concerned with innovation of the process and is willing to change its entire process to minimize the cost of equipment as a whole. This phase would refer to customers completely outsourcing their equipment to a supplier. Customers do not want to own or maintain equipment, they simply want to use it. In addition, they do not want to deal with multiple suppliers.

Phase IV accounts are primary targets for Fleet Management. These accounts are concerned with reducing their cost of process which entails outsourcing all functions not directly related to their primary business. A supermarket chain, for example, has no need to be in the equipment maintenance business. Customers in Phase III are also good target accounts since they are typically under some type of lease-with-maintenance contract. They have already decided they do not want to be concerned with maintaining the equipment they use, now you just need to convince them that they don't even need to have the equipment on their balance sheet.

Phase I and II accounts are probably not ready for a Fleet Management program. When these accounts need new equipment, they are most likely going to negotiate with several vendors to get the lowest price on what they believe to be the highest quality equipment. Your strategy with these customers should be long-term; sell them equipment with guaranteed maintenance, upgrade them to lease-with-maintenance and ultimately convert them to Fleet Management accounts.

The best way to determine buying phase is through a discussion with the customer's purchasing department. If this is not possible, the Consumption Matrix can help to determine the probable buying phase as well as the probable fleet size as mentioned earlier.

Segmenting By Consumption

Using the Consumption Matrix is useful in determining fleet size and buying phase. If these pieces of information are already known, then the matrix can be used to help visualize which accounts you should be targeting for Fleet Management.

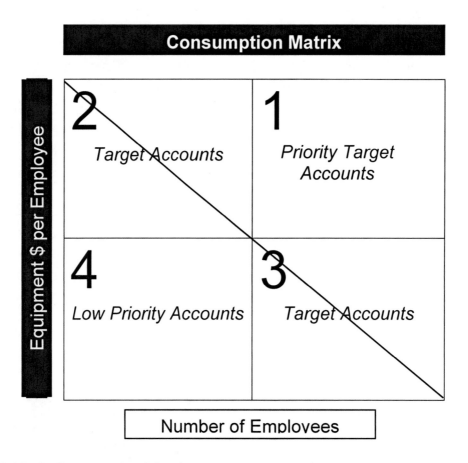

Consumption Matrix

2 Target Accounts

1 Priority Target Accounts

4 Low Priority Accounts

3 Target Accounts

Equipment $ per Employee

Number of Employees

Table 4: Consumption Matrix

The vertical axis (on the left) of the matrix is the amount of money the account spends on their equipment fleet, on average, per employee. This information is frequently available from the manufacturer. The data is broken down by SIC code, so you need to know the account's industry. You can then use these industry averages to plot along the vertical axis. The horizontal axis represents the total number of employees employed by the account, information you should have available internally. Intuitively, companies with a high number of employees and a high dollar per employee expenditure (Quadrant 1) are buying and using the most equipment. Let's look at each quadrant individually.

Quadrant 1

Quadrant 1 contains accounts that have a large number of employees and spend a good amount per employee on equipment. Logically, these will be the largest compa- nies in our database. Upon segmenting our account list into this matrix, you will find that the "A" accounts will generally fall into Quadrant 1. You should also find that

Quadrant 1
Priority Target Accounts
• A Customers • Phase IV Buying • Fleet Manage- ment Candidates

many of these customers have evolved to Phase IV. Their large fleets and sophisticated purchasing processes make Quadrant 1 accounts our primary candidates for a Fleet Management pro- gram.

Quadrants 2 & 3

Quadrants 2 and 3 are very similar, but there are important distinctions. In both Quadrants, you should generally find "B" and "C" customers. The diagonal line through each Quadrant represents the break between whether the account is a "B" or a "C." Accounts with more employees and greater spending per employee will end up in the upper right part of the Quadrant. They will also have more equipment thus making it a "B" ac- count. Those accounts with fewer employees and less spending will fall into the lower corner of the Quadrant and will tend to be "C" accounts.

> **Quadrant 2**
>
> *Target Accounts*
>
> - B & C Customers
> - Phase III Buying
> - Generally Lease With Maintenance

Accounts in Quadrant 2 have fewer employees, but they spend more dollars per employee on equipment units. In this case, the account probably relies more on equipment functions to keep its operation running. Due to this reliance, these accounts are most likely to be in Phase III where they are concerned with product quality and also the cost of fleet ownership. To reduce costs such as buying and servicing equipment, these customers have turned to lease with maintenance contracts. They want reliable equipment to use in their operations; they do not want to be in the Fleet Management business. These are good target accounts because they will have decent sized fleets and should be moving closer to becoming Phase IV accounts.

> **Quadrant 3**
>
> *Target Accounts*
>
> - B & C Customers
> - Phase IV Buying
> - Generally Guaranteed Maintenance

Quadrant 3 accounts have a lot of employees but spend less money per employee on equipment. Because equipment tends not to be critical for these companies to continue operating, and because they operate a number of units, these accounts are still focused on buying a premium product at a low price. They are not as concerned about the entire process (i.e. they are in Phase II). They are likely to have purchased guaranteed maintenance on their units, but they probably still purchase the units as opposed to leasing. You may not be able to sell Fleet Management to these accounts right away, but they are good targets for lease with maintenance contracts. You can then develop the account into a Fleet Management contract as they progress through Phase III and into Phase IV.

Quadrant IV

Finally, you should find that most "D" customers will land in Quadrant 4. Quadrant 4 represents low usage companies with few employees. These are generally Phase I and a few Phase II accounts; it would take a large time investment to develop them to Phase III or IV, and even if you were successful, these accounts may not provide much of a return due to their size.

Quadrant 4
Low Priority
Accounts
• D Customers
• Phase I Buying
• Approach with telemarketing

You will want to approach accounts in Quadrant 1 first. Then the dealer needs to make a decision about which Quadrant 2 and 3 accounts to target. This decision should be based on the dealer's strategy toward account acquisition and development. You don't want to ignore Quadrant 4 accounts, but at the same time it is difficult to justify allocating our limited resources to calling on such customers. It would probably make more sense to utilize telemarketing and/or direct mail to contact them.

All of the accounts you identified in the first step of this process should now be segmented as Phase I, II, III or IV and be assigned to Quadrant 1, 2, 3 or 4. There are probably too many accounts in Quadrants 1, 2 and 3 for the dealership to cover all of them effectively. The next step is to decide which of the target accounts you should pursue most aggressively.

Prioritizing Accounts

The account segmentation process has been relatively quantitative up to this point. Now you need to make some decisions about how you are going to decide which accounts to call on. Just because an account falls into Quadrant 1, 2 or 3 does not necessarily mean it is a high priority account for the individual dealership; it merely means that the account is likely a good candidate for Fleet Management. This step needs to take into account the dealership's strategy and resources.

Table 5: Account Prioritization Matrix

		Account Prioritization Matrix		
		Priority		
Quadrant (From Consumption Matrix)		High	Medium	Low
	1			
	2	*Place account names in boxes*		
	3			
	4			

In this step, you take each account listed in Quadrant 1 and assign it a high, medium or low priority ranking. This is repeated for each Quadrant. The next question is what is, or should be, a high, medium or low priority?

Some factors to consider:

- Location/Distance From Dealership
- Application/Usage
- Amount Of Service Purchases/ Maintenance Contracts
- Credit Rating
- Growth Potential
- Is The Fleet Standard Or Highly Customized?
- Do They Lease Or Buy?
- How Long Have They Been In Business?
- How Loyal Has The Customer Been?
- Financial Situation

One approach the dealer may want to use is to assign a weight to each of the factors listed above. As an example, consider the following:

Table 6: Priority Weights

Factor	Weight	Factor	Weight
Location/Distance		**Credit Rating**	
• 1-50 Miles	3	• Good	3
• 51-100 Miles	2	• Fair	2
• 101 + Miles	1	• Poor	1
Application		**Growth Potential**	
• Easy	3	• 10% +	3
• Moderate	2	• 5-9%	2
• Severe	1	• 0-4%	1

You can assign weights to each factor you consider important – feel free to add to the ones listed here – based on the strategy and priorities of your business. Once this is done, you can add all of the weights. The highest totals represent the highest priority accounts. These accounts can then be plotted according to the priority you just assigned and the Quadrant they fell into in the Consumption Matrix. The following are descriptions of typical high, medium and low priority accounts.

High Priority Accounts

A high priority account is generally one where the dealer already has a relationship and has been working to become the account's single-source provider. The customer is in close proximity to the dealership or a branch (50 miles or less) so they are easier to serve, have good credit with us (paying within 30 days), and run their businesses professionally ensuring continuity of the account. The application will be a relatively easy one requiring standard equipment.

Medium Priority Accounts

With medium priority accounts, the dealer usually has a relationship but is not the dominant supplier. Because these customers shop for the low price, they may have 4 or 5 competing product lines in the fleet. They use the equipment in moderately severe applications and require some amount of customization. This customer is a little farther away (50-100 miles) making them more difficult to serve, they pay their bills in a reasonable amount of time but not as quickly as you may like, and they are not always professionally run, meaning they may not be in business in 10 years.

Low Priority Accounts

A low priority account is just seeking the lowest price making it difficult to hold any kind of margin. They will shift suppliers routinely, are far away from the dealership (150 miles +), pay their bills rather slowly, and are poorly managed. They might be using the equipment in severe applications requiring mostly customized units. These customers would be in Quadrant 4; you might deal with them if they come to us.

These are guidelines: the dealer has the ultimate decision about which accounts best fit with the overall strategy. After all the names of the accounts have been placed in a box, it becomes clearer which accounts you are going to want to target, but there are still decisions to be made. For instance, while it is clear that "High" priority "Quadrant 1" accounts are the top priority, our number two priority accounts may be divided among "Medium" priority "Quadrant 1" and "High" priority "Quadrant 2". The remainder of the chart is read in the same way.

Summary

Gathering information about and compiling a database of all the accounts in your area were described. Also discussed was how to segment these accounts on the basis of size, buying phase and consumption. Finally, how to prioritize the accounts in such a way that you are targeting those accounts that are most likely to be receptive to your sales efforts and Fleet Management was covered.

The next phase is to actually approach these accounts. Chapter 2 describes how to decide on an appropriate approach strategy based on the information you have available about a particular account and the dealership's resources and ability level.

2. Approach Accounts - (Sales Action Plan)

Overview

Once the target accounts have been identified, an appropriate entry strategy must be determined. Four strategies are outlined here, along with guidelines on implementation. The choice of strategy or combination of strategies will be dependent on the strengths and depth of your sales force, the amount of information already known about the target account, and your dealership's experience with Fleet Management accounts. In addition, the attitude of the account toward Fleet Management and other specific circumstances of the target account will play a role in your choice. The four entry strategies described here are:

- Targeted Presentation - Case Study
- Targeted Presentation - Accumulated Account Data
- Targeted Presentation - Account Change Agent
- Expanded Presentation - Hoshin Program

Dealership Capabilities

To determine the appropriate approach methodology, analyze your dealership in terms of:

Your sales force's ability to sell Fleet Management

The sales team involved in Fleet Management includes the sales manager, after-market managers, dealer principal, and controller, CFO, or accountant. In most cases they will do the majority of the selling on these accounts. However, the entire sales force must have the ability to address the Fleet Management issue. 'Ability to sell' in this case also involves preparing and delivering the kind of individualized presentations necessary for Fleet Management.

If the sales capability is low, no form of Fleet Management selling should be attempted. Instead, work to develop and/or replace your salespeople. If their ability is moderate, the Hoshin Program may be appropriate as an entry strategy because an outside facilitator rather than someone from the dealership does the initial presentation. If the sales capability is high, any of the three targeted presentation strategies may be used, depending on the other dealership and customer characteristics.

The data already accumulated concerning the account

Next review the amount of data you've already collected about the account. If you have collected very little information, the Hoshin Program will be the best methodology because it is not targeted at the specific account. A moderate or extensive level of information will enable you to use one of the targeted methods described.

The dealership's Fleet Management experience

Finally, take a look at the amount of Fleet Management contracts you already have, or how many Fleet Management arrangements you have a good working knowledge of through your manufacturer or another source. A high, medium, or low level of experience will give further insight into the appropriate methodology.

Now examine the capabilities in relation to the chart, and begin to determine the Approach Methodology most appropriate. The minimum requirements to implement a particular strategy are listed below:

Table 7: Dealership Capabilities

APPROACH METHODOLOGY				
DEALERSHIP CAPABILITIES	CASE STUDY	ACCUMULATED DATA	ACCT CHANGE AGENT	HOSHIN PROGRAM
SALESFORCE CAPABILITY	HIGH	HIGH	HIGH	MODERATE
TARGET ACCT DATA	MODERATE	HIGH	MODERATE	LOW
DEALERSHIP EXPERIENCE	HIGH	LOW	MODERATE	LOW

Account Interest

After identifying the possible methodologies based on dealership capabilities, determine how much interest the account currently has in Fleet Management. The interest levels below are the minimum requirements necessary to implement a particular strategy. Based on dealership capabilities and account interest, choose an approach methodology. (More direction on the appropriate level of capabilities and account interest is included within the discussion of each methodology.)

Table 8: Account Interest

	CASE STUDY	ACCUMULATED DATA	ACCT CHANGE AGENT	HOSHIN PROGRAM
TARGET ACCT INTEREST IN FLEET MAN- AGEMENT	MODERATE INTEREST	HIGH INTEREST	INTEREST COULD BE INCREASED BASED ON COMPANY CHANGE	LOW INTEREST

Case Study Presentation

One option in approaching the target account is to design a presentation specifically for that account, centered on the case study of a similar company. That company should be a current Fleet Management customer and have characteristics similar to the target. This strategy should be used if the following conditions exist:

Sales Force Capability: The sales force and sales manager have the capacity to develop individualized presentations and address all levels of the target accounts in an in-depth fashion.

Target Account Data: Enough data has been accumulated about the target account to show similarities between an existing Fleet Management account and the target. If an abundance of information exists about the target account's current fleet, application, and costs, this strategy may be used in conjunction with the accumulated data methodology. If information exists about current changes in the target company, this strategy may be used in conjunction with the account change

> As your number of Fleet Management accounts grows, however, this approach in conjunction with others will become your most effective.

agent methodology. To adopt this strategy alone, only a moderate amount of information on the target account must exist.

Dealership Experience: To successfully execute the case study methodology, the dealership must have some previous experience implementing a Fleet Management account. In fact, the dealership must have enough history with a Fleet Management account to present a variety of benefits that this program brought to the account.

Target Account Interest: To use this methodology, there should be some indication that the account will be open to the idea of Fleet Management. The time involved in creating a presentation specific to the account and getting the account to commit the time to hear it necessitates some moderate level of interest. However, the target account need not be at a specific growth phase, time of change, or size, to be appropriate for this strategy.

The case study methodology will not be appropriate for all target accounts at this time. Even if the dealership has the sales force and experience requirements, not all targets will have enough interest in Fleet Management or similar characteristics to a case history account to warrant this approach. As your number of Fleet Management accounts grows, however, this approach in conjunction with others will become your most effective.

When this strategy is appropriate, first create your presentation. It can take the form of a series of overheads, a computer presentation, a workbook, a video, or a combination of the four. Whatever the format of the presentation, make sure to leave materials with the target account, including the benefits of Fleet Management to the customer in the case history. When complete, the presentation should answer the following questions:

- What are the characteristics of the company? (size, industry, etc.)
- How was the equipment process structured before Fleet Management?
- What made the company decide to use your Fleet Management services?
- How did you analyze their application and costs data?
- How did you estimate your own costs?
- What was the scope and structure of the agreement you reached with the account?
- What were the expense savings that the account experienced due to Fleet Management?

Expense savings can be shown through a cost per operating hour analysis or a total annual cost analysis. To estimate cost per hour savings, use the cost data that you used in your initial analysis of the account's fleet. Direct cost data will probably already be calculated by operating hour. Indirect costs can be shown separately along with the total operating hours and your calculated indirect cost per operating hour. The total of the direct and indirect costs per operating hour should then be compared with the cost per operating hour paid now to your company. The difference is the expense savings incurred.

To estimate annual cost-savings, compare the total cost from your initial analysis of the fleet with the total annual cost the account pays to you now. You will need to summarize differences between the two time periods in terms of fleet size, operating hours, facility size, and other factors that affect a direct comparison.

What was the cash or balance sheet benefit to the account due to a buyback of equipment, a reduction or elimination of parts, and/or a reduction in total equipment needs due to more efficient management and access to the dealership's rental fleet?

What was the uptime benefit to the account of using your Fleet Management service?

This data can be presented through a comparison of average maintenance and repair time before Fleet Management and now, or a presentation of how many low utilization, secondary units the account needed on hand before Fleet Management in order to plan for downtime, if specific uptime data does not exist.

- What other benefits does the account feel that it has achieved through the Fleet Management process?
- What has been the feedback from the account in terms of the Fleet Management process and your dealership in particular?

This information can take the form of direct quotes from the account, information gathered through quarterly reviews with the account, the renewal of the contract, or recommendations the account made of your services.

- What are the similarities that you see between this company and the target account, and how is this case study relevant to the target account?
- What would be the process you would employ with the target account if they expressed interest in pursuing Fleet Management?
- What resources would you need from the target account to complete the process?

A single case study may be used as the basis of presentations for a number of target accounts. However, the similarities between the case study account and the target account will be specific to the target, and openings and closings of the presentations should be individualized. In all methodologies except

Hoshin, be sure to describe in detail what Fleet Management is, what it may or may not include, and how the contracts may be structured. Details in terms of scope and structure can be found in Section V, Structure Proposal. Also include the benefits to the customer listed in the Introduction. Feel free to include the benefits to the dealer and the manufacturer as well to educate the target account as to your purpose.

Accumulated Account Data Presentation

The second option to approach the target account is to design a presentation centered on specific accumulated data of that account, and the benefits the account would enjoy as a Fleet Management account. This strategy should be used if the following conditions exist:

Sales Force Capability: The sales force and sales manager have the capacity to develop individualized presentations and address all levels of the target accounts in an in-depth fashion.

Target Account Data: To successfully execute this methodology, an abundance of data must exist about the account in terms of fleet size, fleet mix, application, costs, and personnel.

Dealership Experience: The dealership needs no previous experience in Fleet Management to use this methodology. However, you need a good working knowledge of the Fleet Management Process and how to determine fleet costs. You also need to be committed to providing Fleet Management if the proposal is sold and the capability to develop an implementation plan and carry it through. If the dealership does have Fleet Management experience, you may use this strategy in conjunction with the case study methodology.

Target Account Interest: Again with the accumulated account data methodology, there should be a good indication that the account will be open to the idea of Fleet Management. The time involved in analyzing current estimated costs creating a presentation specific to the account necessitates a good level of interest. If you know that the target is going through a change that would make them more receptive to outsourcing, you may use this strategy in conjunction with the account change methodology.

That sort of change may be a drastic increase in size due to an acquisition, merger, etc., or a decrease in size that forces cost cutting procedures. It may be a change in top management or the operations management in charge of company equipment. Finally, the account's industry may be changing at a rapid pace, or the account may have begun outsourcing other functions. However, the target account need not be at a specific growth phase, time of change, or size, to be appropriate for this strategy alone.

The accumulated data methodology will not be appropriate if the sales force is already overextended, or if the target account is not open to the idea of Fleet Management. More importantly, this strategy will only be successful if there is a good amount of accurate information. Ideally, the following information will be known about the account's equipment process to create the presentation used in this methodology:

- Application Data
- Industry
- Operating Conditions
- Operating Area
- Operation Severity
- Driver & Supervision Information
- Floor/Yard Information

- Equipment Duty Cycle
- Acquisition Cost Data
- Depreciation Expense of Fleet
- Interest on Fleet
- Lease Payments
- Rental Payments

- Original Acquisition Cost of Older Units
- Usage Cost Data
- Equipment:
- Operator Training
- Fuel
- Service
- Technician Wages and Benefits
- Tools and Supplies
- Training
- Supervisor Salary and Benefits
- Parts

- Inventory & Ordering Personnel Wages and Benefits
- Inventory Expense
- Pilferage
- Administrative Cost Data
- Purchasing Personnel Wages and Benefits
- Human Resource Personnel Wages and Benefits
- MIS Expense
- Purchase Order and Payment Processing Expense

Obviously not all of the data will be known. However, Chapter 3, **Performing Customer Analysis**, will give you guidelines on estimating some of the cost information. Based on the level of information accumulated, the presentation can take one of the three forms.

First, if the majority of data points can be identified or esti-mated, analyze the data and develop a total cost summary as described in Chapter 4 – **Developing Pricing**. Then develop an estimate of your cost to provide the Fleet Management neces-sary. The presentation must make it clear that the analyses are estimates based on data that may or may not be complete. However, make the information as accurate as possible. Then point out estimated cost-savings based on a specific proposal scope and profit expectation of the dealership.

Preparing this presentation is very similar to the process of preparing a proposal, so all of the guidelines set forth in this book should be examined prior to beginning. You must also be quite sure that the account will be open to listening to your presentation, as the material is specific to them and cannot be used for any other targets. However, if you are successful in 'selling' a situation analysis, this entry strategy will save time during the subsequent steps of the process. The data already accumulated need only be verified, and analyses need only be adjusted after data collection is complete rather than beginning from scratch.

If application and direct cost data is known or can be estimated, but indirect cost data is unknown, develop an estimate of the total direct cost to the account. If you have done other cost analyses for companies, use that information to give an example of an indirect cost load for the sake of this presentation. Calculate the percent of indirect costs to direct costs for all cost analyses you've completed. Then show the range of percents, the average of the percents, and any data specific to the industry of the account you're targeting. Complete the presentation as in option 1 with savings to the target account contained in an example of a proposal and with a specific scope and profit expectation built in.

If you have not completed other cost analyses, do not include the indirect cost analysis in your presentation. Instead, develop the estimate of your total cost and compare it to the account's direct cost structure. In all probability, your cost will still be lower. Then list in your presentation all the indirect costs that you would determine during a situation analysis. Complete the example by showing that even with a minimal or nonexistent indirect expense load (depending on the difference between your estimated cost and their direct cost) and an appropriate dealership profit worked in, that the savings to the account would be meaningful.

Obviously, this analysis will take some manipulation of the total cost structure. The goal is to demonstrate cost-savings to the account, to interest them in a situation/needs analysis.

However, they also must understand that eliminating indirect costs will add substantially to their savings, and that the dealership must calculate in an appropriate level of profit.

The third scenario is that application information is known, but direct cost information is limited. If you know the number and type of equipment, use industry data to estimate the direct cost of the current fleet. Then follow the steps of option 2 to devise a presentation that represents an average scenario for that fleet size and mix.

Obviously this strategy in conjunction with an actual case study will be extremely effective, as you develop more Fleet Management experience and cost information. Conversely, it will also be the most time consuming strategy because it is so individualized. Consider the time to be an investment in the future of the industry, but also keep track of the time it takes to create these presentations when determining an appropriate profit level.

Account Change Agent Presentation

The third option is to approach the target account with a specific presentation based on a change that the account has recently experienced. That change could be a significant change of size due to downsizing, merger, or acquisition. It could be company relocation or a significant change in the industry. The change could involve personnel changes, especially top management or operational management. Finally, the company may have started outsourcing other processes, which constitutes a significant change in the way it does business. This strategy should be used if the following conditions exist:

Sales Force Capability: The sales force and sales manager have the capacity to develop individualized presentations and address all levels of the target accounts in an in-depth fashion.

Target Account Data: Enough data must exist about the account to devise a meaningful targeted presentation. That presentation can center on a case study or on individual account data. However, it must incorporate both of those elements to some extent. Fleet size and mix and application data at a minimum must exist.

Dealership Experience: The dealership must have some previous experience or knowledge of Fleet Management accounts in order to create a meaningful presentation. That presentation may center on a case study or on individual account data, but it must incorporate both elements to some extent. The dealership should also have some previous experience working through a company change process, either internally or with a customer. That experience will improve insight in the process.

Target Account Interest: The target account must be anticipating, experiencing, or have just experienced a significant change such as those explained above in order for this methodology to be appropriate. The account's interest in Fleet Management may not be known in this case, as many of the changes cited imply unknown personnel in decision making positions at the account. If your sales force can generate enough interest within the target account to schedule a presentation, there is enough interest to adopt this strategy.

The account change methodology will not be appropriate if no change agent exists. In addition, if even the most minimal account fleet information cannot be obtained, or if the dealership cannot obtain a moderate amount of information about existing Fleet Management accounts, a presentation cannot be developed.

When a change agent exists, the focus of this presentation should be to show why this is an opportune time to enter into a Fleet Management contract. Because each change agent brings about its own specific presentation arguments, these presentations will be unique to the change. Here are guidelines to use for the most common change agents.

Significant Size Increase

Suddenly the account has a much larger group of equipment to manage. Time and expense to research increasing the fleet (if the size increase is due to growth in business) or how to integrate two existing fleets (in the case of a merger or acquisition) must be considered. In addition, the cost to maintain the fleet will increase. The first issue the presentation should address is timing. Due to the change and the burden of an increase in equipment needs, this is an ideal time to outsource Fleet Management. In fact, if a merger or acquisition is the cause of the increase, outsourcing this system will reduce conflict in terms of decision making between two existing systems.

Once the argument has been made that this is the right time to outsource based on non-financial reasons, you must show the potential financial benefit to the target account. Here you can center the presentation around a similar case study or on accumulated account data. Or, because much of the sales technique here is the benefit of outsourcing because of the size increase, you can create an example of cost-savings under similar conditions, rather than using an actual case or actual data. With basic knowledge about cost analyses for Fleet Management contracts and the application and fleet size information of the account, create a realistic expense load for the account. Point out the expense increases that will or have occurred due to the size increase. Examples:

- Increased number of service technicians if service is done in-house - In addition to the hourly compensation for these technicians, include a benefit load, extra insurance and taxes the company will incur, the cost of extra managers or supervisors to oversee them, training, tools, and repair space.
- Increased parts inventory if service is done in-house.
- Increased number of invoices due to the additional equipment, repairs, and maintenance.

The cost of the increased invoices could include an increase in accounting personnel and increased computer system needs. At the least, an hourly expense for processing the invoices will be incurred.

Increased secondary units will be needed on hand for downtime coverage.

Once you've presented an example case, show how Fleet Management can save the account the costs of investing in the larger fleet, parts inventory, and service staff. Present the benefits of your planned maintenance and accessible rental units to minimize downtime. Finally, reiterate the benefits of having an outside firm managing the process to maximize utilization and profitability, and free up management staff to other core aspects of the business.

Significant Size Decrease

Suddenly the account has to downsize and has a need of less equipment to manage. They have extra units that need to be sold, and a cost saving is increasingly important. In this case, the cost saving elements from any method described earlier can be utilized (case history, accumulated data, or cost-saving example). In fact, there should be savings to them immediately by outsourcing and ongoing savings of the actual contract.

Point out the savings of outsourcing service if they have been doing it in-house. At this point, their technician productivity would decrease if fewer units were being used, and it would no longer be efficient (if it ever was) to maintain a service team. In addition to extra equipment, they may also have extra parts in inventory. Offering to buy back these assets can infuse the company with some much-needed cash at a time of crisis. Finally, overhead personnel such as service managers, inventory managers, and invoice clerks can be minimized if Fleet Management is outsourced.

Note that a company suddenly downsizing may be in a precarious financial situation. A long-term contract with a financially unstable company should be approached with caution. On the other hand, if there is a decrease in equipment needs because of a shift in business mix or a partial relocation of the company, the financial health may not have changed.

Company Relocation or Significant Industry Change

When a company relocates, it is the perfect opportunity to reexamine existing processes and design new, more efficient methods. In fact, with all the changes surrounding the move, a company is often grateful to have an outside firm take charge of specific company functions. Similarly, when there is a significant change in an account's industry, the account is already destined to change significantly. In this circumstance, there is so much uncertainty in terms of functions, processes, and the like, that a non-core process can be a real burden to the account.

In both cases, the account needs flexibility and high performance from all facets of the company. Center your presentation around the ease with which you can serve their ever-changing needs in a cost-saving way. Incorporate one of the methods to show cost-savings described earlier, but focus in on the minimal effort they need to exert for you to obtain the data you need to develop your proposal.

Personnel Changes

When a company changes top management personnel, new ideas are especially welcome. New management wants to demonstrate their worth to the company immediately and are expected to make changes. In this situation, long-term profitability of the company will be key. By demonstrating the on-going cost-savings of Fleet Management, you'll capture their interest.

Unlike a downsized company, where a short-term infusion of cash may be the real selling point, in this case new management will want to build the long-term profitability of the company. When developing the cost analysis and the savings to be realized, use a longer-term example rather than just a one-year contract. Demonstrate how annual savings add up to 'x' amount through five years. In addition, without the units and parts inventory on the books, the balance sheet of the company is improved. Minimizing costs and debt add to the long-term outlook of a company, potentially increasing the stock value of a public company.

Note that not all personnel changes will be permanent, and some company cultures may resist change despite the new personnel. However, approaching the company at this time is still advantageous in many cases.

Operational Changes - Outsourcing

When a company begins outsourcing other functions such as accounting, payroll, personnel, training, purchasing, cleaning, sales and marketing, etc., you have a prime opportunity for the Fleet Management approach. At that point, you know that the company is open to the idea and understands the potential benefits. In addition, the company probably already has or will soon implement a process by which to analyze, hire, function with, and review outsourcing services.

Because of these accounts' purchasing maturity, they will be ideal target accounts. At the same time, they will have experience with contract options and negotiation points and will be the most demanding accounts. For this group, indirect cost-savings will be extremely important, as will contract options in terms of contract scope and pricing structure. They will understand the benefits of fewer invoices and parts inventory and will want more specific information concerning those 'soft' data points. They will also want to negotiate specific points and you will do well to have several options to present.

Be clear in your potential cost-savings example, and list specifically the data points you will use in your situation analysis. Be prepared for them to insist on an 'open book' policy (your books of course!) if they accept the proposal. Also be prepared to learn something from this group of target accounts. The experience of dealing with several outsourcing industries will be found here and could give you additional strategy and analysis ideas for the future.

Hoshin Program

Finally, if none of the previous approach methodologies are appropriate, approach target accounts through the group presentation found in the Hoshin Program. This program is designed to address the needs of accounts in all four buying phases, not only Phase IV, Fleet Management. This strategy should be used if the following conditions exist:

Sales Force Capability: The sales force and sales manager do not have the capacity to develop individualized presentations or address all levels of the target accounts in an in-depth fashion. Current coverage may be very low, or the capacity for analysis and development of presentations may be limited to a very few target accounts.

Target Account Data: The only data that exists about accounts is their address, the contact name, and that they are an equipment user.

Dealership Experience: The dealership needs no experience with Fleet Management to conduct the Hoshin program.

Target Account Interest: The target accounts must simply be open enough to improving their equipment process that they agree to attend the seminar.

This strategy is not appropriate if one of the other approaches can be used. It is not specific to Fleet Management and does not address the target account individually. After running the Hoshin program, it is expected that individual follow-up with Fleet Management target accounts will center on the Fleet Management portion of the Hoshin seminar.

Refer to the Hoshin Program Section in the rear of the book- Dealer Procedure

What is Hoshin Kanri?

The image most often depicted in U.S. literature on Hoshin Kanri is that of a ship's compass distributed to many ships, properly calibrated such that all ships through independent action arrive at the same destination, individually or as a group, as the requirements of the "voyage" may require.

Hoshin Kanri is a systems approach to the management of change in critical business processes using a step-by-step planning, implementation, and review process. Hoshin Kanri improves the performance of business systems. A business system is a set of coordinated processes that accomplish the core objectives of the business. For every business system there are measures of performance and desired levels of performance. Hoshin Kanri provides a planning structure that will bring selected critical business processes up to the desired level of performance.

http://www.mcts.com/Hoshin-Kanri.htm

Book for the details on running the Hoshin Program. In brief, the program's purpose is to penetrate specific accounts that will increase revenue and profit percent for the dealer network and the manufacturer. The entry strategy to those accounts is a half-day seminar planned and marketed by the dealer, facilitated by a third party presenter. Seminar participants will be taught the four phases of product maturity in equipment applications and identify their current phase.

For each phase the facilitator or manufacturer will present a description of the analysis methodology. Therefore, participants will begin to understand the way in which the dealer methodologies could help them analyze their current needs, leading to either innovation or improvement of the existing process. The review or control step for each phase will then be discussed, along with a PMI evaluation (the Pluses, Minuses, and Interesting aspects of each phase).

Finally, for each phase, the dealership will be expected to present at least one case history in which a customer in that particular buying phase either innovated or improved its equipment management process. Details on how to develop and present the case history material is included in the section of the Hoshin Program Book on preparing seminar materials.

Summary

The four entry strategies outlined here included three targeted presentation approaches and one group presentation approach. To determine which methodology is appropriate, examine four issues: sales force capability, target account data already compiled, the dealership experience with Fleet Management, and interest in Fleet Management of the target account. Once a methodology has been determined, prepare the presentation and execute the approach. If there is interest in going forward, you can now schedule a customer analysis. If the account is not interested, return to evaluating an appropriate approach methodology. On a regular basis, attempt a different strategy until a customer analysis can be scheduled.

3. Performing Customer Analysis - (Sales Action Plan)

Overview

Once the customer has been sold on the idea of Fleet Management, the dealer must begin the process of gathering necessary data about the customer's fleet. This chapter describes what types of information need to be gathered from the customer, where to find the information and how to develop reasonable estimates when critical data is unavailable. There are three main objectives when performing the customer analysis:

- Determine the account's current cost structure.
- Gain consensus on the cost analysis.
- Gather enough data so that you can:
    - Determine the appropriate fleet size and mix.
    - Develop a competitive and profitable pricing structure for providing the fleet services.

To achieve these objectives, you must complete three steps. First, you must gather information about the customer's fleet operation. Second, you need to obtain the customer's costs for operating the fleet. Finally, you must develop a presentation based on the preceding data which will be used to gain consensus between the dealer and the customer around the cost analysis. Each of these phases is outlined in this chapter.

Gather Fleet Operation Data

Equipment Application and Operation

The first step in analyzing a customer's fleet is to determine what the units are used for and under what conditions they operate. You first want to know what industry the customer is in, what specific equipment is needed and how it is used. This information will give the dealer some insight as to the composition of the equipment fleet and how critical each unit is to normal operations.

You also want to know the types of conditions that are present within the customer's facilities. Some of this will be clear based on the industry, while other information needs to be obtained through observation or interviewing managers and employees. Knowing the operating conditions will help the dealer to better estimate equipment life, types and frequency of repairs and which equipment models are best suited to the customer's needs. Questions that need to be considered are:

- Is the facility or application clean or dusty?
- Is it wet or dry?
- Is the unit around explosives, abrasives or corrosives?
- Is extreme humidity present?
- Are there extreme hot or cold temperatures (as in freezer storage or foundries)?
- What percentage of the unit's operating time is spent under the temperature extremes?
- What are the maximum summer and minimum winter temperatures?
- What is the height of the ceiling or racking, if any?
- What type or types of racking is in use?

Knowing the customer's industry will address many of these points, but there are additional factors relating to how the customer's facility is designed and maintained. For instance:

- Do the units operate primarily indoors or outside?
- Are the units used on trailers, boxcars, mines, elevators etc.?
- How is the operating area maintained (is it swept frequently or rarely)?
- How many hours are there of continuous operation for the average equipment?
- What unusual conditions does the equipment operate in?
- What is the typical load carried?
- What type of flooring or surface do the units operate on?

Almost all of these questions can be answered rather quickly through observation during a walk-around tour of the customer's facilities. There is some additional information that will require the dealer to do some research in the form of interviews with supervisors and managers.

You will want to know how many shifts the units are run as three shifts will require PM's closer together than one shift. You should also find out how many hours per shift the fleet is used. Knowing the number and hours per shift will also give you the information you need to estimate the running hours per year for the entire fleet.

The plant manager(s) should be able to tell us what, if any, seasonality exists within their business. This can also be acquired through an examination of the customer's revenue stream over the past two or three years. If the customer is unwilling to share this data, aggregate information on particular industries is available from a variety of sources including:

- The Internet: Hoover's Online (www.hoovers.com)
- Dun and Bradstreet (www.dnb.com)

The U.S. government publishes a number of resources that are available at most libraries as well as on the Internet.

Many plants and warehouses have a one or two-week shut down period each year, especially if their industry experiences seasonality. This is important to know because shutdowns can be a valuable time to perform fleet maintenance and, in the longer term, to help the customer improve their overall equipment management process through plant and operation modifications.

Next you want to obtain certain information about the equipment operators. This step will need to be a combination of interviewing managers, supervisors and operators and observing the operators performing the work.

The managers or supervisors should be able to tell you how many drivers are employed at the site. You also want to know what type of training has been provided for the operators, whether they are assigned to a particular unit, how many different drivers operate each unit, and whether the operators are under any type of incentive plan for performance, safety, etc. The dealer should try to make a determination about the quality of operator supervision as well, as this will impact driver performance. If the manager is unable or unwilling to discuss this aspect of fleet operation, the dealer should try to observe plant operations and make a subjective determination based on his observations.

This information is important because the operator has a significant impact on the useful life of the unit. It is important that you understand the skill level of the operators so you can get a sense of how much training should be provided should you sell the Fleet Management contract to the customer. Improving the efficiency and safety of the operators can lead to significant savings to the customer through reduced equipment down-time, fewer accidents and injuries, a reduction in repairs resulting from equipment abuse and improved productivity.

Once all of the information discussed up to this point has been accumulated, the dealer should be able to make a reasonably certain determination as to the severity of the customer's operations. Again, this step is very important as it will ultimately lead to your recommendation to the customer as to how many and what types of units will be most effective in this particular application.

Current Fleet Mix and Condition

You next need to find out what types of equipment are in the customer's fleet and how they have been maintained. For each unit the dealer should collect the following data:

- Manufacturer
- Model
- Serial number
- Year of manufacture
- Hour meter
- Is it operative?
- Original or replacement
- Reading
- Fuel type

- Tire type
- Attachments
- Condition of unit
- Estimated annual running hours
- Is the unit suited for the operator currently running it?

Using this information in conjunction with the application data you collected in part one, you can begin to formulate a picture of what the proper fleet mix should be based on the customer's needs and operating conditions. The dealer may want to request all of the invoices, leases and rental agreements for the fleet as these documents should contain much of the information listed above. These documents will also be useful when you get to the customer cost phase of the program.

Six Sigma

Literally, refers to the reduction of errors to six standard deviations from the mean value of a process output or task opportunities, i.e. about 1 error in 300,000 opportunities. In modern practice, this terminology has been applied to a quality improvement methodology for industry.

http://www.balancedscorecard.org/basics/definitions.html

The final piece of information to collect is the service history of each vehicle. If the dealership has been performing the maintenance, this information should be available to the dealer internally. If the customer is performing maintenance internally or outsourcing to a dealership other than you, the hope is that the customer s have tracked the service history themselves. The reality is that this is often not the case. Request all the service and maintenance invoices that that the customer has for the fleet and build a service history for each vehicle as best you can.

Gathering Customer's Cost Data

In this phase of the customer analysis, the dealer needs to collect actual costs from the customer. This information will be used from a sales approach to illustrate to the customer how Fleet Management will save them money. You will also use the data to develop our pricing structure and to put together our proposal to the customer. There are three major categories of costs incurred by a customer: acquisition of the units; costs related to usage; and administrative costs related to managing the fleet. All costs should be collected for an annual period.

Customers will not always have complete or accurate data on their fleet costs, so it may become necessary to estimate these costs for the customer. When you are forced to estimate try to keep the cost estimate conservative. You may end up with an underestimated fleet operating cost figure, but this scenario is preferable to overestimating and having the customer reject your estimate. It is easier to gain consensus with a conservative figure. For each piece of information, the assumption is that the dealer is requesting the data from the customer. You provide recommendations for developing an estimate in those situations where the customer is not able to provide certain data.

Acquisition of Fleet

These are the costs related to actually getting the equipment into the operation. Units may be purchased outright, leased or rented. Depending on the method of acquisition, there are two ways to find these costs.

For purchased units, determine the depreciation and interest on the units still being depreciated and financed. For purchased units over five years old, assign a cost to them that will indicate an eventual replacement cost. You also need to calculate the opportunity cost involved in tying up capital in equipment units.

For leased or rented equipment, determine the payments for each unit on an annual basis.

Depreciation

The acquisition cost of purchased units still being depreciated will include the amount of depreciation taken on the equipment each year. If you were to just use the actual purchase price of the equipment, you will find that, due to the cyclical nature of new unit purchases, our figure will be incorrect. Depreciation data should be readily available from most customers. If it is not available, the dealer should estimate the cost of each unit based on industry experience and calculate depreciation using a five-year straight-line depreciation method. In some industries and applications, longer depreciation periods may be appropriate.

If the unit is no longer being depreciated, use 20% of the original purchase price as one portion of the acquisition cost.

Interest

For units still being financed, know the amount of interest the customer is paying related to the financing of the unit. That figure should be included in the total acquisition cost. If the customer cannot provide this figure, estimate the interest based on the amount still being financed and a reasonable interest rate (such as the rate you are currently paying on financed units).

Lease and Rental

For those units that are not owned, there should be rental or lease agreements which will indicate the monthly payment for each unit. If this documentation is not available, base your cost estimate on what the terms would be for a comparable unit based on the customer's situation.

Opportunity Cost of Investment

This category takes into account the value of the customer's investment in equipment. If the customer owns the fleet, the capital tied up in the units is not providing a return. If the customer leases, rents, or signs up with a Fleet Management contract, that capital currently tied up in the fleet can be invested in other ways. The customer's opportunity here is the amount of cash obtainable for the fleet multiplied by their internal rate of return – IRR. That is the return they expect from investments and the benchmark to which they compare their investment opportunities. Multiply the total wholesale value of the fleet by the IRR to calculate an approximate opportunity cost of the capital. If you don't know the customer's IRR, use 12% (or another reasonable return).

Total Acquisition Cost
- Total acquisition cost is then the total of:
  o The year's total depreciation on fleet units
  o 20% of the original purchase price of units no longer being depreciated
  o The total interest expense on fleet units for the year
  o The total of lease and rental payments made on fleet units during the year
  o The opportunity cost of owned units as calculated above

Table 9: Current Acquisition Cost

Expense	Description	Estimate (If actual data is not available)
Depreciation: Units still depreciated:	The total amount of depreciation taken for the year	Use original purchase price of equipment and assume 5-year straight-line depreciation to find yearly depreciation taken per unit. Then sum to get total for fleet.
Units no longer depreciated:	20% of original purchase price	Estimate original price based on knowledge of similar units.
Interest:	Amount of interest paid on units for the year	Use prime rate or reasonable rate for customer conditions multiplied by the amount financed.
Lease or Rental:	Payments made for each leased or rented unit	Use terms that you would use for a similar customer leasing or renting a comparable unit.

Expense	Description	Estimate (If actual data is not available)
Opportunity Cost:	The value of the capital that is tied up in the customer's fleet	Multiply the wholesale value of the fleet by the customer's internal rate of return or 12% to get the opportunity cost of the capital invested in the equipment fleet.

Use of the Fleet

Certain costs are ongoing and are related to the customer's use of the units in the fleet. These costs are associated with one of three categories: equipment usage, service or maintenance costs and parts costs.

Equipment

While all of the fleet costs ultimately relate to the equipment units themselves, you break out unit costs as those that are associated with the operation of the unit. That is, what costs are incurred by the unit physically running? The cost categories here are operator wages and benefits, operator training, fuel, and supervisor salary and benefits. Although you give instruction here for calculating all of these costs, if you have no intention of offering a particular element in your Fleet Management contract, there is no need to collect the data.

Operator Wages & Benefits

You will probably not provide operators in the Fleet Management contract, but if you reduce the fleet size you may also be able to reduce the number of operators thus saving the customer money. Therefore, it is important to consider the labor costs involved with the persons actually operating the units. The total wages and benefits should be available from the customer through their W2 filings or income statement personnel breakdown.

To estimate total operator wages for the year, determine how many operators there are in total, or estimate one operator for each regularly used unit. Use the following calculation to estimate total wages:

- Estimate average operator wage through industry knowledge or use standard $15/hr.
- Hours paid per year = 40 hours/week x 52 weeks = 2,080 hours/year
- Average Operator Wage = average wage x # of hours = $31,200/year
- Total Wages = # of operators x average operator wage = 50 (operators) x $31,200 = $1,560,000

To estimate total benefits, use 20% of the total known or estimated operator wages. The cost of benefits for the drivers in the preceding example would be:

Wages ($1,560,000) x 0.20= $312,000/year benefits cost.
Total annual wages and benefits in our example are:
$1,560,000 wages + $312,000 benefits = $1,872,000

Operator Training

You have to consider in the total cost of running the fleet the cost of providing ongoing training to the operators. If the customer cannot tell us how much they spend for training each year (if anything), estimate that each operator should receive 4 hours of training per year. From your own experience training operators, estimate how many operators can be trained at once, and therefore how many hours of a trainer's time the total annual operator training will take. Multiply that by the average charge for training in your area (or $20/hr.) to estimate training costs.

Fuel

While you will likely exclude fuel from the Fleet Management contract, you want to know the customer's fuel costs because if you install more fuel-efficient units and/or reduce the fleet size, the customer's fuel costs will drop. If the customer cannot provide this total, you will need to estimate the cost.

Know the fuel type for each unit in the fleet. If you estimate the number of running hours each unit will get on a tank of fuel or power charge, then divide this figure by the total running hours per year, you know how many tanks of fuel each unit will consume, or charges are needed. Multiply the total number of tanks by the appropriate price per tank (this may vary based on the type of fuel) and you have a fuel cost estimate.

Supervisory Salaries and Benefits

Finally, you have to consider supervisory salaries and benefits into the cost of running the equipment. The customer should be able to provide the supervisor's salaries. If they do not track the cost of benefits, use the 20%-of-salary estimate you used in the Operator Benefits section. If the supervisor is also an operator, you just leave his salary and benefits under the "operator salary and benefits" category as you will be totaling all of these costs in the end anyway.

- Total Equipment Usage Cost
- The total usage cost related to the units is then the sum of:
  - Annual operator wages and benefits.
  - Annual cost of operator training for all operators.
  - Annual fuel cost for all equipment.
  - Annual salaries and benefits of all supervisory personnel.

Table 10: Current Usage Cost - Equipment

Expense	Description	Estimate (If actual data is not available)
Operator Wages & Benefits	Total of wages and benefits paid to equipment operators	**Wages:** Use typical wages for an equipment operator in your area. (Check with local unions) **Benefits:** Assume an additional 20% of total wages for the operators' benefit load.
Operator Training	Amount paid to trainer or for seminars related to ongoing safety or operational training of operators	Assume 4 hours of training per driver per year, a typical number of drivers trained at one time, and a cost of $20 per hour.
Fuel	Cost of gasoline, diesel, propane etc.	Use estimated # of running hours a unit will get from 1 tank of fuel. Divide the annual running hours by this estimate to arrive at the number of tanks required per year. Multiply the number of tanks required by the appropriate price per tank for each fuel type.
Supervisor Salary & Benefits	The total compensation paid to all of the supervisors/ foremen/ managers that oversee the equipment operators.	Assume the operator supervisor earns approximately the same as a dealership service manger. Add 20% of salary for the benefit load.

Service

In order to keep the units running, customers have to fix the units when they break. They should also be performing routine maintenance (oil changes, adjustments etc.) to avoid unplanned downtime. Therefore, the service cost of using the fleet is the total labor cost of repairs and maintenance for the year.

Continuous Improvement

Focuses on improving customer satisfaction through continuous and incremental improvements to processes, including the removal of unnecessary activities and variations.

If the customer out-sources equipment service to a local equipment dealership, determine how much was paid to the dealership for service. This should be available from the accounts payable department or by reviewing the fleet service history obtained at the end of the previous section. If this is unknown, refer to a program like a Maintenance Rate Calculator and determine the approximate service cost for each unit.

If the customer performs service internally, the cost categories are technician wages and benefits, technician training, supervisor salaries and benefits, tools and supplies, occupancy expense, and the cost of downtime.

Technician Wages and Benefits

The cost data required here is the total wages and benefits paid for each technician dedicated to equipment service. If technicians work on other machines, obtain an estimate of the percent of their time spent on this equipment, and use that percent of wages and benefits as your cost number.

If the customer does not have the data, then the estimate calculation will be identical to the one performed above in "Operator

Wages and Benefits." However, you may want to use our own dealership' average service technician wage as an estimate.

- Estimate average technician wage through dealership data: $15/hr.
- Hours paid per year = 40 hours/week x 52 weeks = 2,080 hours/year
- Average Technician Wage = average wage x # of hours = $31,200/year
- Total Wages = # of technicians x average wage = 50 (operators) x $31,200 = $1,560,000
- Then add the 20% for benefits to obtain the labor cost per service technician.

Technician Training

Similar to the "Operator Training" category, you want to find out how much is spent for ongoing training for technicians. If you have to estimate this cost, you can assume three days (24 hours) of training per year per technician, or use the amount of training your average technician participates in. Estimate the number of hours a trainer must be paid for, and multiply the number of hours by a trainer cost. If your dealership offers training, use your standard rate. If you don't offer training, then use the rate that your dealership pays for a trainer. Otherwise, estimate $20 per hour per technician for training.

Supervisory Salary and Benefits

This will be a similar calculation to that For "Operator Supervisory Salaries and Benefits". Again, you might get a better estimate here by using the dealership's service supervisor or manager's salary as a benchmark. Add the 20% benefit load and multiply by the number of service supervisors employed by the customer.

Tools and Supplies

This category will include all customer-purchased tools and all of the supplies needed in the service department. The tools cost will consist of the amount spent to acquire or replace tools this year. For large equipment (lifts, hoists, etc.) or tools purchases (such as the original purchasing of all the shop tools) that are considered capital expenditures as opposed to being expensed, use the amount of depreciation taken this year as the cost of these items. In the event that this is not readily available, follow the methodology you used to estimate equipment depreciation under "Acquisition of Fleet."

Supplies should include office supplies, lubricants, uniforms, rags, cleaners etc. These expenses should be included in the operating expense detail of the service department budget. If you can not get specific information regarding supplies expense, estimate based on the costs of supplies in the dealership service department and adjust this amount based on the volume of the customer's service department. For example, if your dealership performs 1,000 repairs a year (based on the number of work orders), and the customer performs 200 repairs a year in his service department, you might use 20% of our own supplies cost as an estimate of the customer's supplies cost.

Occupancy Expense

If the customer is performing service in-house, there must be space allocated as a service area. You have to consider this occupancy as a cost of the fleet since, if the customer outsources service, this space can be used for additional production capacity. If the customer has not tracked the service area occupancy expense you can estimate based on the square footage of the service area(s) and the customer's cost per square foot of the facility. If the service area is 2,000 square feet and the customer pays $5 per square foot per month for his lease, then occupancy expense will be $120,000 per year.

Cost of Downtime

Unplanned downtime costs money. Ideally, you want the service department to maintain the fleet in such a way that downtime is minimized so when a unit does go down unexpectedly, you allocate the cost to the service department. Even if you outsource service to a dealership, downtime costs are still going to be incurred from time to time. The major component of this cost is in terms of lost productivity. Consider the following:

If the units are critical to the operation, a breakdown could costs thousands of dollars an hour in lost productivity.

There may be an operator without a unit during the breakdown if no backup is available. Consider the cost of his unapplied time.

If the customer utilizes rental units to cover downtime, the cost of the rental unit will be included in the cost of downtime.

If the customer has backup units, there may not be any cost to one unit going into the service shop. If there aren't backups, then determine how many unscheduled breakdowns occurred in the last year. If the customer does not track this himself, you will have to examine the units' service histories and/or service work orders to estimate how much time was spent on repair (you will assume all maintenance is performed on a schedule and does not result in unplanned downtime).

If at all possible, the dealer should also try to separate breakdown repair from abuse repair. This will give some idea as to how well operators are trained and how the units are treated. It will also give a selling point when you present the cost analysis;

if you are going to provide for operator training in the Fleet Management contract, you can show the customer the potential savings (in terms of abuse repairs) resulting from having better trained operators.

There is no accurate way to estimate the customer's cost of losing a unit from production unexpectedly. If equipment is critical to the customer's operation, this cost could be very high, but you will have to rely on the customer's estimate. Estimate the cost of using a rental unit to replace the broken one if the customer can not give us this information. Simply use your dealership's short-term rental rate for a comparable unit in a comparable application.

You can also estimate the cost of an unapplied operator by taking the average hourly operator wage and multiplying by the number of hours of downtime. If you are paying $15 per hour for the operator to move product around the facility, then you can assume that it is costing us $15 per hour of downtime for the operator to be unapplied since you still have to pay the operator's wages, but no work is being accomplished. Remember that this assumes that there are no backup units available and the operator is simply idle until his unit is back online.

Total Service Usage Cost

The total usage cost related to servicing the equipment is then the total paid to an outside source for the labor involved in servicing the fleet, or the sum of:

- Annual technician wages and benefits, equal in percent to the portion of time spent on the equipment fleet
- The cost of technician training for the year
- Annual supervisor salary and benefits
- The cost of tools and supplies for the year, relative to the servicing of the fleet
- The occupancy expense related to the service area
- The cost of downtime related to unplanned repairs on the units
- If some service work is done internally and some is done by an outside source, add together the price paid externally with the calculation of internal cost above.

Table 11: Current Usage Cost - Service

Expense	Description	Estimate (If actual data is not available)
Technician Wages & Benefits	Total of wages and benefits paid to service technicians for work done on fleet	**Wages:** Use the average tech wage for dealership technicians multiplied by the number of hours and number of technicians. **Benefits:** Add 20% of total wages for benefit load
Technician Training	Amount paid to trainer or for seminars related to ongoing technical training of service technicians	Multiply 3 days per year per technician at the rate charged by the dealership (if dealership offers training). Otherwise assume the amount that the dealership pays for training or use $20 per hour. Divide the total by in the number of techs that can be trained at one time.

Expense	Description	Estimate (If actual data is not available)
Supervisor Salary & Benefits	The total compensation paid to all of the supervisors/ foremen/ managers that oversee the service techs	Assume the service supervisor earns approximately the same as a dealership service manager. Add 20% of salary for the benefit load.
Tools & Supplies	The total amount paid for tools, equipment and supplies used by the service department	**Purchases treated as capital expenditures:** Use depreciation amount as annual cost. Estimate depreciation using 5-year straight line depreciation based on original purchase price of equipment. **For expensed purchases:** Use the amount the dealership service dept. spend on these items, then adjust based on the difference in service volume.
Occupancy Expense	The cost of the space utilized by the service department (bays, offices, storage)	Determine the square footage utilized by the service function and multiply by the customer's rent or lease cost per square foot.
Cost of Downtime	The cost (generally in lost productivity) to the customer as a result of unplanned equipment downtime	**Cost of rental unit used to fill in for broken unit**: Use dealer's typical rental rate for comparable unit. **Cost of operator's unapplied time:** The hourly wage of the operator multiplied by hours of downtime.

Parts

If the customer pays for service to be done on the fleet outside the company, the cost of parts will be the total parts figure from all invoices that year.

If the customers have an in-house service department, they need to purchase parts. In addition to the cost of the parts, there are other costs associated with parts acquisition, namely, inventory carrying expense, parts personnel, supplies, and inventory storage (occupancy).

Inventory

You need to know how much the customer has spent on parts for the fleet. This can be obtained from the customer's accounts payable department or by examining the service work orders. If you need to estimate parts costs, you can take two approaches. If there are a reasonable number of units in the customer's fleet (under 50 for instance), refer to a program such as a manufacturer's maintenance history or experience and look up the approximate parts consumption by unit. For competitive brand units, or if it is a very large fleet, find information from industry standards per unit per year in parts consumption.

Inventory Carrying Expense

The customer will also incur costs relating to carrying parts inventory if they do not order parts as-needed from suppliers (i.e., a "just-in-time" parts system). This figure can be calculated by taking the total value of the parts inventory (wholesale or book value can be used) and multiply this by the customer's internal rate of return. If the customer's IRR is unavailable, use a reasonable return such as 12%. This figure represents the return the customer is foregoing by tying up capital in parts inventory and could also be referred to as the opportunity cost of the investment in parts.

Consider the cost of insurance to cover parts inventories and any property tax that must be paid on the value of the inventory at year-end. If the costs aren't available, estimate them by taking the total tax and insurance expenses related to inventory (if available), and multiplying it by the percent of total inventory that parts represents.

Personnel

For a customer with a very large fleet, there may be personnel dedicated to ordering and maintaining parts inventory. If this is the case, obtain the wage and benefit expense for these employees.

If there are dedicated parts employees, but you cannot obtain accurate information about their wages, use the dealership's employees as the basis for your estimate. If the customer has multiple parts employees, use the dealership's parts manager salary and benefits to estimate the customer's parts supervisor salary. For other employees, base your estimate on the rate paid to the parts clerks in your dealership. If you just have salary information, don't forget to add the 20% benefit load to this figure.

Supplies

Supplies should include office supplies and forms used in the parts department. These expenses should be included in the operating expense detail of the parts department budget.

If you can not get specific information regarding supplies expense, you may want to estimate based on the costs of supplies in our dealership parts department and adjust this amount based on the volume of the customer's parts department. For example, if our dealership orders 10,000 parts a year (based on the number of purchase orders), and the customer orders 2,000 parts a year through his parts department, you might use 20% of our own supplies cost as an estimate of the customer's supplies cost.

Occupancy Costs

As in the service department, you want to determine the cost of the space occupied by the parts function. This will include storage facilities and any office space required for parts employees. To estimate this cost, if necessary, determine the square footage of the aforementioned parts space and multiply by the cost per square foot that the customer pays for his facility. Remember to consider the space required to store any equipment fuel that may be kept on the premises.

Total Parts Usage Cost

The total usage cost related to providing parts for the units is then the total paid to an outside servicing organization for the parts, or the sum of:

- Cost of parts inventory used internally.
- The carrying cost of keeping a parts inventory on hand.
- Annual parts personnel salary and benefits.
- The cost of supplies for the year, relative to supplying parts for the fleet.
- The occupancy expense related to the parts area.

If some service work is done internally and some is done by an outside source, add together the price paid externally for parts with the calculation of internal cost above.

Table 12: Current Usage Cost - Parts

Expense	Description	Estimate (If actual data is not available)
Inventory	Cost of the parts either from a supplier or to an outside service provider	Depending on the size of the fleet, refer to a Maintenance Expense Calculator or find an industry average per unit per year.
Inventory Carrying Expense	Costs related to tying up capital in parts inventory	Multiply the value of the parts inventory (wholesale or book value) and multiply by the customer's internal rate of return or 12%
Personnel	Total of wages and benefits paid to dedicated parts department personnel	**Wages:** Use the average wage for dealership supervisor or clerk, depending on which position you are estimating. **Benefits:** Add 20% of total wages for benefit load
Supplies	The total amount paid for supplies used by the parts department	Divide your dealership's cost of supplies by the dollars of parts bought per year. Apply that same percentage to the customer's parts purchases.
Occupancy Expense	The cost of the space utilized by the parts department (bays, offices, storage)	Determine the square footage utilized by the parts department and multiply by the customer's rent or lease cost per square foot.

Total Usage Cost

Total usage cost is then the total of:

- The year's total equipment usage cost
- The total cost of servicing the fleet for the year
- The total cost of supplying parts for the fleet for the year

Fleet Administration

These are the remaining expenses that are difficult to assign to a specific fleet function but are incurred as a result of operating the equipment fleet. These costs are often buried in the administrative functions of the entire company and not quantified when the customer tries to determine the total cost of his equipment management function. This is because many of these functional areas serve the entire organization, not just the equipment fleet. Our task here is to try to estimate what portion of the purchasing, human resources, MIS and payables departments resources are utilized by equipment management.

Purchasing

The purchasing department is typically responsible for pricing materials and choosing the suppliers for the organizations. The cost of purchasing is the amount spent for personnel, operating, and occupancy expenses related to purchasing the fleet. Generally, a company will know its total cost related to the purchasing department. If they also know the amount spent on equipment for the year, divide that by the total for a percent figure. Multiply that percentage by the total cost of purchasing to estimate their purchasing expense for the fleet.

If the information is not available to perform this calculation, use the following data obtained through a manufacturer's research. The time involved in capital appropriations is approximately 47 hours per location. Therefore, take the number of locations the customer has and multiply it by 47 hours. Obtain the average salary for the customer's purchasing personnel and divide by 2080 hrs (or estimate $25/hr.). Multiply the cost per hour by the number of hours involved in capital appropriations.

Human Resource Expense

Consider the percentage of the human resources function that is expended on fleet employees. Rarely will specific personnel be assigned solely to equipment management. Therefore, you will most likely need to estimate this figure.

To estimate, take the total number of employees at the customer's location and divide by the number of human resource personnel. This will give us the employee to HR personnel ratio. Then, adding up all of the fleet employees – operators, technicians, parts personnel and supervisors –figure out how many human resource people are needed for the fleet operation. Multiply the number of HR people by the average salary (use the national average of $33,500 if the customer's actual figure is unavailable), add the 20% benefit load if it is not already included, and this will be the fleet operation's portion of HR expense.

Purchase Order & Payment Processing

The cost of generating purchase orders and checks for payment can be surprisingly high. Research has found that it cost about $90 per purchase order and $60 per check in administrative costs. When you consider the fact that customers may be making lease and/or rent payments each month and are generating purchase orders and cutting checks to suppliers/vendors at least monthly, customers are spending a lot of money in this area. When the dealer implements Fleet Management, the customer sends one check per month or per quarter to the dealer which covers all (or nearly all) of his fleet expenses.

Check with the purchasing and payables departments to see if they already have information on the number of checks and purchase orders they process for the fleet operation each month. If the customer cannot tell us, you can determine the customer's cost by finding the number of checks and purchase orders generated in an average month and multiplying by $60 or $90, respectively. It could be tricky to estimate the number of checks and POs generated, but you can come up with a ballpark estimate by filling in the following chart.

Benchmarking

Benchmarking is using standard measurements in a service or industry for comparison to other organizations in order to gain perspective on organizational performance.

For example, there are emerging standard benchmarks for universities, hospitals, etc. In and of itself, this is not an overall comprehensive process assured to improve performance; rather, the results from benchmark comparisons can be used in more overall processes.

Benchmarking is often perceived as a quality initiative.

Assume that you need to generate one P.O. and one check per vendor per month.

Payee	# of Months	Checks		Purchase Orders	
		Number	@ $60 Each	Number	@ $90 Each
Leasing Vendor	12	12	$720	12	$1,080
Parts Vendor	12	12	$720	12	$1,080
Service Supplies	12	12	$720	12	$1,080
Fuel Supplier	12	12	$720	12	$1,080
Other	12	12	$720	12	$1,080
	Total	*60*	*$3,600*	*60*	*$5,400*
				Annual Total	**$9,000**

Table 13 Illustration of Purchasing

The actual totals may well be significantly higher than this estimate. If the customer has to make just one monthly payment to the dealer, and not generate monthly purchase orders, he can ultimately save the himself $8,280 per year.

Other Costs

There are two other costs that are difficult to estimate if the customer does not track but that can be significant: MIS and pilferage.

There is certainly some type of management information system in use by the customer. The cost of entering fleet information into the system, generating reports and possibly customizing the system to handle fleet tracking should be obtained if possible.

Finally, account for tools and supplies pilferage by employees. Again, while often overlooked, replacing stolen tools and supplies can be a large expense burden for a customer. It may be difficult to quantify this expense if the customer does not track it since it would be hard to discern which tools and supplies were replaced due to wear vs. those that were replaced because they disappeared. You should still attempt to bring this factor to the customer's attention, however.

Total Administration Cost
- Total administration cost of the fleet is then the sum of:
  - The year's total cost of purchasing of the fleet
  - The cost of human resource functions relative to the fleet for the year
  - The annual cost of purchase order and payment processing
  - The year's MIS and pilferage costs relative to equipment management

Table 14: Current Administrative Cost

Expense	Description	Estimate (If actual data is not available)
Purchasing	Cost allocated to the fleet function for the use of purchasing department resources (negotiating with vendors, processing POs, etc.)	Multiply the number of customer locations by 47 hours. Obtain the average salary for the customer's purchasing personnel and divide by 2080 hrs (or estimate $25/hr.). Multiply the cost per hour by the number of hours involved in capital appropriations.
Human Resources	Percentage of the human resource function that is utilized by the fleet operation	Divide the total fleet employees (operators, technicians, parts personnel, supervisors) by the total company employees to get what percent are fleet employees. Apply this percentage to the total wages paid to human resource personnel (use $33,500 if actual is unavailable). Add 20% benefit load if not already included.
Purchase Order & Payment Processing	The total cost of generating purchase orders and payments related to fleet operation purchases.	Determine the number of POs and checks generated (refer to tables in the text). Multiply number of POs by $90 and checks by $60.
Other costs	Costs associated with pilferage and MIS usage for the fleet operation.	Get costs from customer if they have estimates. Otherwise, determine these costs to the best of dealer's ability.

Calculate Total Customer Cost per Hour

When all acquisition, usage, and administrative costs have been calculated or estimated, add them together for a total annual cost of the fleet. In itself, although it will be of interest to the customer, the total has little value to you. In order to compare that total with industry data or the price you can offer for Fleet Management, you must present the cost data relative to the fleet size and application.

The most common way to do this is by calculating the cost per operating hour of the fleet. When you collected application data, you should have collected the hours per unit. From service logs and other data available through the customer, you should be able to estimate the number of operating hours for the year for each unit. Add them together and divide the operating hours into the total cost calculated for cost per hour figure.

If actual operating hours cannot be estimated, use your industry knowledge to estimate the hours per unit given the number of shifts run, the type of unit, the application, etc. In the next section, you'll compare the current cost per hour to the industry averages to begin creating your sales presentation.

Gather Customer's Business Projections

Once you have compiled the customer's costs, forecast the costs based on the customer's business projections. Obtain the customer's volume and revenue projections for the next five years. If the customer doesn't have projections, or won't share them with you, research industry projections to estimate their revenue increase, or use a standard 5% increase.

If the customer is planning for 10% revenue and volume growth per year, you need to assume that their equipment management spending will increase as well. Therefore, you want to emphasize to the customer that while their costs today might be $1,000,000 per year, for example, they might be $1,100,000 next year, $1,210,000 the second year and so on.

Next, you want to compare the customer's equipment costs per hour (total fleet costs as calculated above divided by hours of operation) to their industry average. Your manufacturer may have this data available for a number of industries. You can then develop a chart similar to the following:

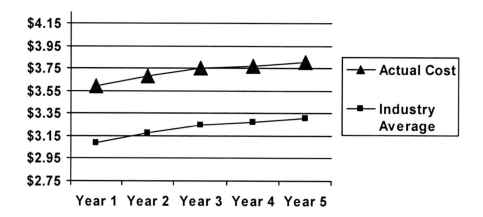

It should be noted, however, that industry data may not include all of the costs included here. In particular, most of the administration costs and operator costs will probably not be included. Find out from the source of the industry data what is and is not included, and compare it with the customer's data that corresponds. You can then show the additional cost categories that are not included in the industry data.

If the customer is spending more than the industry average, our proposal becomes even more important in that you can show the customer how to bring them in line with and even below industry spending thus eliminating any cost disadvantage they had been dealing with. If you can even beat the industry average, you can actually provide the customer with a cost advantage. Be careful about presenting the above chart if the customer is already below the industry average as they may feel that they are doing well enough. They may not realize the full potential of outsourcing their fleet.

Present and Gain Consensus on Cost Analysis

Once you have gathered the necessary cost data and compiled it using a spreadsheet program, sit down with the customer to explain and discuss the findings. This step is critical; the dealership should be represented at this meeting by the dealer principal, the sales manager, the service manager and the controller or CFO. From the customer team, arrange to have the operations manager, the general manager, the controller and anyone interviewed in the analysis process present at this meeting. It is at this point where you begin to sell the savings that Fleet Management offers the customer.

Hopefully you will have received much of the cost data directly from the customer. In this case, consensus will generally be easier to achieve. When the dealer has had to make a number of estimates, the consensus stage could become more of a negotiation. The customer may be hesitant, especially in the area of administrative costs, since these are less obvious and generally more difficult to quantify. When the customer does raise an issue with the data, the dealer team needs to explain the methodology and work towards agreement on each cost item individually.

The dealer should prepare a presentation to present his findings to the customer. Be prepared to explain each category where you have had to estimate the costs. It is recommended that the dealer format the presentation in the same way that the analysis is discussed in the text, breaking costs into acquisition, usage and administrative. This will provide a logical flow through each cost category as many of the later cost data builds on that acquired earlier in the process.

If you are unable to gain consensus at this initial meeting, you go back and reinvestigate the disputed items. You may need to do additional research and take the customer's feedback into consideration in modifying our presentation.

Summary

You have walked through the steps for acquiring a complete customer analysis from gathering information on the fleet and its applications to obtaining or estimating all the costs associated with operating this fleet. Once you are able to achieve consensus on this analysis with the customer, you are ready to begin developing our price estimate for the contract.

4. Developing Pricing – (Sales Action Plan)

Overview

After performing the customer analysis, you must determine the appropriate fleet mix and size for the account, what it will cost you to manage that fleet, and what your appropriate profit level should be. This section discusses:

How To Determine The Appropriate Fleet

- How to determine the appropriate cost to the customer of acquisition of that fleet, based on the dealer attaining the benchmark gross profit level
- How to determine the appropriate usage cost to the customer of the fleet, in term of equipment, service, and parts, based on the dealer attaining the benchmark gross profit level
- How to determine the administrative cost to the customer based on the dealer attaining the benchmark performance level
- What factors to take into consideration when determining the appropriate cost-savings to offer the customer

Note that when you estimate costs in this section, you calculate them as annual and monthly totals. It is also appropriate to show cost per operating hour. Simply divide the annual cost by the estimated number of operating hours.

Determine Appropriate Fleet

Now that you've gathered the customer's application data and direct information about the fleet, you can make some assumptions about the size and appropriateness of the current fleet. You can also use the customer's business projections to estimate the upcoming fleet needs.

Are the units appropriate for the job? Analyzing the current application data, does the customer use the most efficient type of units for the job? Are there new models that could do the job better? Will a different size or capacity unit increase the efficiency of the process?

If the current equipment models are appropriate, is the fleet size appropriate? How many hours did each unit operate last year? How many shifts did the customer run? How much unused time was due to repairs and maintenance how much was necessary because of the process and how much was due to overcapacity (too many units in the fleet)? How many units are kept in the fleet to cover downtime and seasonal increases?

Do current business projections warrant maintaining overcapacity in the fleet? Using the customer's projections, see if the volume of equipment investment increasing substantially over the next year? If so, how should you alter the fleet to accommodate the increase?

In most cases, either through incorporating more appropriate units for the job or by maintaining an effective maintenance cycle, the customer's fleet can be reduced. There are two ways to look at reducing the fleet. The first is to identify particular units from the existing fleet that aren't used enough to warrant their ownership and eliminate them. The second option is to determine the required productive hours for each type of unit, and calculate the appropriate number of units. Following is an example of each method.

Method I: Separate the units by capacity and list the information below for each unit for the current year. Identify units that may be eliminated based on the information attained.

Table 15: Fleet Determination Method

Unit	Year	Hours Down due to Maintenance	Hours Down due to Repair	Hours Run (A)	Hours Available (B)	Utilization (A ÷ B)	Other Reasons for Low Utilization
01	02	3	10	300	2067	15%	Used primarily as backup
02	07	5	20	800	2055	39%	Used primarily during peak season
03	01	3	40	1700	2037	83%	Process constraints
04	04	8	25	1800	2047	88%	
TOTAL		19	95	4600	8206	56%	

In this example, a closer examination of units 01 and 02 is warranted to determine whether one of them can be eliminated. In a Fleet Management situation, placing unit 01 or 02 into the dealership's rental fleet and accessing the unit only during the peak period might be optimal. In addition, if the three units kept are properly maintained, they may suffice even for that peak period.

Method II: The second method for effectively downsizing the fleet is to estimate the number of running hours needed for a particular type of unit and then determine how many units are necessary. Using the example above, for that particular type of unit, you need the following:

Table 16: Fleet Determination Method II

Estimated Hours Needed – Regular	Estimated Hours Needed – Peak & Backup	Estimated Hours Repair & Maint. per Unit	Estimated Hours Available per Unit	Units Needed – Regular	Units Needed – Seasonal Supplement
3500	1100	30	2050	?	?

Using the information above, it's easy to calculate that 2 units are needed for regular use. Discussion with the client will determine how many units should be brought in to supplement the fleet during the busy period, when that period is, and how long it will last.

When using either method, be sure to note any situation where the customer is especially sensitive to downtime. In some applications, downtime cannot be tolerated, in which case a backup unit should be available. In other cases, the customer may be located far away, making it especially difficult to service the unit unexpectedly. In those cases again, a backup unit might be beneficial from a financial and customer expectation viewpoint.

Benchmark Performance

The appropriate price to charge the customer for the fleet should be based on the revenue necessary to attain benchmark performance. Benchmark performance for your dealership as a whole is a minimum 5% net profit. The relevant financial benchmarks for each business segment are as follows:

	Unit Acquisition	Rental	Service	Parts	G&A
Revenue	100%	100%	100%	100%	
Cost of Goods Sold	85%	55%	35%	65%	
Gross Profit	15%	45%	65%	35%	
Total Expenses	85% of GP	20%	35%	15%	10%
Net Profit	15% of GP	25%	30%	20%	-10%

Table 17: Financial Model

Expect a 15% gross profit for units, a 65% gross profit on service work, and a 30% gross profit on parts. These are the financial levels that you control through the price you charge for Fleet Management. Then if you manage the account correctly, as discussed in Chapter 7, expect a net profit at the levels shown above (15% of unit gross profit, 30% of service revenue, and 15% of parts revenue).

These levels of business segment profit are necessary to pay all normal general and administrative expenses related to the revenue. The resulting net profit should be between 5% and 10%, depending on the fleet mix.

In addition to the normal costs and expenses taken into account by the financial benchmarks, Fleet Management contracts incur the added expense of training operators and administrating the contract. In the following sections, the various cost segments to the customer of a Fleet Management contract and how to price them within the boundaries of these financial benchmarks will be discussed.

Determine Acquisition Cost

Definition: <u>**Acquisition Cost**</u> – is the price that the dealer must charge for supplying the units themselves. This cost to the customer covers the dealer's cost of the units (acquisition and financing) and the gross profit the dealer must charge to attain the benchmark performance.

Permanent Fleet Units

Although the units will already be in place at the customer site, you will be buying them from the customer, and leasing them back to the fleet. Assume that the cash involved in the transaction will dictate that you finance the units. Therefore, although many of the units may be old, assume that you will be financing them at your current interest rate.

Also note that the units should bring you the normal 15% gross profit expected on new units. That profit is necessary to cover all sales expenses associated with the Fleet Management contract. Thus the acquisition cost of the units is a straightforward calculation. Now that you've identified the fleet necessary to service the account:

- Identify the cost of each unit, assuming you would buy them new.
- Calculate the monthly payments of a five-year financing deal, using the interest rate you're currently paying.
- Calculate the 15% financial model gross profit expected on new units and divide by 60 months.
- Add together the monthly financing cost and the monthly gross profit expected.

Example:

Table 18: Acquisition Cost

Model	Cost to Dealer	Interest Rate	Monthly Cost to Dealer (A)	15% Gross Profit	Monthly Gross Profit _(B)	Total Acquisition Cost to Customer (A+B)
XXXXX	$20,000	8%	$405.53	$3,530	$58.92	$464.45

The resulting acquisition cost is the amount that should be acquired from the customer simply for the unit. In your contract, you'll be stating a replacement schedule. This payment cycle will cover your acquisition costs regardless of how often the units are replaced

Rental Units

If you have determined that some rental units will be used during peak seasons, calculate the cost of those units using the following process:

- Determine the current acquisition cost of the rental units needed.
- Multiply the acquisition cost by the 5% Short-term Rental Monthly Revenue Multiple.
- Multiply that monthly revenue figure by the number of months each will be used to obtain the annual rental cost. Add that cost to the regular fleet acquisition cost when developing your Fleet Management price.

Estimate Usage Costs

Definition: **Usage Costs** - are defined as those costs accumulated through running the equipment. They can be separated into those related to the equipment, service, and parts. Usage costs are calculated here at the price that must be charged to the customer to attain benchmark performance.

Equipment

The usage costs of the equipment can be separated into costs that are usually covered under a Fleet Management contract, and those usually not covered. In most cases, the dealership will not supply the operators for the equipment, so costs related to operators will not be included in your pricing. Also, fuel is not usually included in the contract, but your choice of fuel-efficient units will be a benefit. Therefore, request fuel expense data on an on-going basis to track the customer's expense savings in that area.

If your customer requests the inclusion of these items, add them into the analysis below.

Costs usually not covered under Fleet Management
- Operator Applied and Unapplied Wages
- Operator Benefits
- Supervisor Salary & Benefits
- Fuel

Costs covered under Fleet Management
- Operator Training

Although operator training will decrease the repair cost on the units and is therefore a benefit to the dealership, training should not simply be given away as part of the Fleet Management contract. The OSHA requirements for operator training mandate the customer acquire the training, so a value must be assigned.

Guidelines on developing operator-training schedules are discussed elsewhere in this book. Depending on the size of the fleet, the complexity of the machines, and the number of operators, estimate the amount of time on an annual basis that training will take. If you already have a retail rate established for training, use that as a basis for the contract pricing. You may negotiate the pricing later in the process. If you don't have a rate established, consider the cost in wages and benefits of the trainer for the time training, preparing, and traveling. That should be the minimum charge, and a mark-up can be applied. With that information, the following steps can be taken to obtain a monthly equipment usage cost per unit:

- Determine the number of operators and total number of training hours per year needed.
- Multiply the training hours by the assigned billing rate to determine the total annual cost of training.
- Divide that cost by twelve months to determine the total monthly cost.
- Divide the monthly cost by the number of units in the fleet to assign a cost per unit per month.

Step 1:

Table 19: Equipment Usage Costs

Number of Operators/ Number of Units	Annual # Hours Standard Training	Annual # Hours Specialty Training	Annual Total Training Hours	Billing Rate	Annual Cost	Total Monthly Cost	Monthly Cost per Unit
	(A)	(B)	(A+B=C)	(D)	(CxD=E)	(E÷12=F)	(F÷60)
50/60	20	5	25	$85	$2,125	$177	$2.95

Service

- Applied and Unapplied Labor
- Tools & Supplies
- Training & Technician Benefits
- Cost of Downtime
- Supervisor Salary & Benefits
- Occupancy Expense of Service Bays

Based on a standard Fleet Management contract, all of the above expenses will be incurred by the dealership except for the downtime expense. The dealership's costs are the same as that for all service work performed. Therefore, the goal is to estimate the number of service hours to be spent for each unit on an annual basis, and bill it at the full retail rate:

- Estimate the number of PM's to be done on the unit based on the estimated running hours.

- Estimate the service hours to be spent on PM's based on the number of PM's and the average time per PM.
- Multiply the total time for PM's by the full retail rate to obtain an annual <u>Labor Cost of PM's</u>. The full retail rate should be 3.5 times the average technician wage, leading to a gross profit of 65%.
- Estimate the repair time necessary to service the unit this year. Many manufacturers have programs available to help estimate the cost per hour of each unit. These various programs will all give you guidelines in terms of cost per operating hour.
- Estimate the cost per year by multiplying the estimated number of hours to be run this year by the cost per hour. Make sure that you're using your full retail rate for the calculation of <u>Labor Cost of Repairs</u>.
- Based on the number of PM's and the approximate number of repairs to be done on the units, estimate the travel time involved in servicing the unit. Remember that several units should be serviced each time out, and factor that in. (If 6 PM's can be performed in 1 day, divide the travel hours by six for each unit.) Multiply the travel time by the full retail rate to obtain the <u>Cost of Travel</u>.
- Add together the cost of PM's, repair, and travel to get the total annual service cost for each unit. Divide by twelve for the monthly service cost.

Example:

Table 20: Service Usage Costs

Model: XXXXX - Estimated Hours: 1500				
# of PM's	Hours Spent on PM's (A)	Billing Rate (assumes a 65% GP) (B)	Annual Labor Cost of PM's (AxB=C)	Monthly Labor Cost of PM's (C÷12)
4	4	$85	$340	$28.33
		Repair Cost per Operating Hour[3] (A)	Annual Labor Cost of Repairs (Ax1500 hrs.=B)	Monthly Labor Cost of Repairs (B÷12)
		$0.83	$1,245	$103.75
Round Trip Travel Hours to Customer	PM's Done per Visit/Travel Hours for PM's[4]	Annual # of Repairs/ Travel Hours for Repairs	Annual Cost of Travel[5]	Monthly Cost of Travel
1	6/.67	4/4	$396.95	$33.08
Vehicle Travel 80 miles round trip				
4.67 trips x 80 miles x $1.50 per mile = $560.40 ÷ 12 =				$46.70
				Total Monthly Service & Travel Cost
				$211.86

---

[3] Based on the equipment, the base hourly repair cost will change. But if the expected cost was $1.25 per running hour, you also know that generally the labor is 2/3 of the cost and the parts 1/3. Here you are only looking for labor costs.

[4] 1 hour travel per PM visit ÷ PM's done per visit = .17 x 4 PM's annually = .67 hours for each PM.

[5] 4.67 total travel time x $85 billing rate = $396.95 annual cost of travel

Parts

- Inventory Expense
- Personnel
- Ordering/Inventory Management System
- Pilferage
- Occupancy Cost

As with service, the total expense of parts based on usage of the fleet should be covered by the normal gross profit. Therefore, if you charge the full retail rate for parts, all personnel, operating, and occupancy expenses will be paid, and a net profit will be earned. The process for estimating parts expense is:

- Obtain an estimate for parts consumption on each unit, based on class and unit data from your manufacturer or other sources.
- If that consumption figure is at cost, calculate to achieve the financial model 35% gross profit.

Example:

Table 21: Parts Usage Costs

Model	Average Annual Parts Cost (A)	35% GP (C-A)	Total Annual Parts Cost (A÷.65=C)	Monthly Parts Cost (C÷12)
XXXXXX	$420	$225	$645	$53.75

Total Usage Cost

Table 22: Total Usage Costs

Monthly Training Unit Cost	Monthly Service & Travel Cost	Monthly Parts Cost	Total Usage Cost to Customer
(from Table 20)	(from Table 21)	(from Table 22)	
$2.95	$211.86	$53.75	$268.56

Estimate Administrative Cost

Definition: **Administrative Cost** is the price that the dealer must charge for overseeing the Fleet Management contract. This cost to the customer covers personnel, operating, and occupancy expenses relative to contract, not included in the units, service, and parts segments of the business.

The administrative costs of running a fleet include:

■ Purchasing
■ Human Resources
■ MIS
■ Accounting and Processing Functions
■ Tracking Expenses and Reporting

In a Fleet Management contract, the dealership will perform all of these functions, although the customer must still process payments. By charging the customer the financial model rate for units, parts, and service, the dealership is covering their normal G&A expenses of units, parts, and service. Any additional services included in the contract that are not normally incurred, however, must be calculated.

The expense of tracking contract costs separately is the most obvious additional administrative burden in Fleet Management contracts. In addition, a management person to oversee the account or a group of accounts may be necessary. As you become experienced with these contracts, you'll be able to estimate these costs easily. In the meantime, simply calculate a management fee of 5% to the total of the acquisition and usage costs.

Example:

Table 23: Administrative Costs

Total Acquisition Costs	Total Usage Costs	Total Acquisition and Usage Costs	5% Administrative Fee
(from Table 19)	(from Table 23)		
$464.45	$268.56	$733.01	$36.65

Calculate Total Cost

Definition: **Total Cost:** is the sum of all cost categories described in this section. It is expressed as the cost to the customer for the Fleet Management contract described, at a level consistent with benchmark performance for the dealer.

Cost per Unit

In the sections above, you calculated each set of costs separately at the model financial performance level. That individual calculation is important to get the most accurate estimates of cost based on the application of the units, their ages, services histories, etc. In the example, total cost of that one unit is:

Table 24: Total Unit Cost

Total Acqui-sition Costs	Total Usage Costs	5% Administration Fee	Total Unit Cost
(Table 19)	(Table 23)	(Table 24)	
$464.45	$268.56	$36.65	$769.66

When giving the customer an initial estimate before all data is collected, however, the following rule of thumb may be used:

Determine the acquisition cost of the unit:

- Multiply it by the Long-term Rental Monthly Revenue Multiple of 3.5%.
- The resulting figure is minimum revenue to be obtained for acquisition and usage costs.
- Add to that figure the 5% administration fee.

This method is fairly accurate in average application settings, but adding a 10% cushion to the estimate is advisable. The example above would yield approximately a $35 difference between the two methods.

Table 25: Costing Method Comparison

Revenue Multiple Method		Detailed Costing Method	
Acquisition Cost (Table 19)	$20,000	Acquisition Cost (Table 19)	$464.45
Revenue Multiple	3.5%	Usage Cost (Table 23)	$2668.56
Acquisition and Usage Costs	$700	Acquisition and Usage Costs	$733.01
5% Administration Cost	$35.00	5% Administration Cost (Table 24)	$36.65
Total Unit Cost	$735.00	Total Unit Cost	$769.66

Cost per Fleet

To estimate the entire annual cost and financial return for each contract, estimate the costs for each unit. Then add the fleet totals together, including any rental units that will be necessary for seasonal use. Calculate the net profit attained from each contract segment

The following example is of a 60-unit fleet where the average unit costs are equal to the example you've used throughout this section. The following conditions apply:

- The appropriate costs to the customer as stated throughout this section were achieved, leading to the model gross profit levels shown.
- The Fleet Management contract is run at model levels, leading to the model net profit for each segment.
- The standard G&A level of 10% of service and parts revenue was spent on G&A for the sales, service, and parts segments of the contract.

- The usage cost of the units (operator training) and the administrative fee will pay for the services provided, but will have no profit value to the dealership.
- No seasonal rentals are necessary.

Table 26: Fleet Cost and Profit

	Cost to Customer at Model Performance Level	GP % to Dealership	Net Profit Percent to Dealership	Profit $ to Dealership
Acquisition Cost	$295,186	15%	15% of GP, or 2.25% of sales	$4,860
Usage Costs:				
Units	$1,000	0%	0%	0
Service	$140,098	65%	30%	$42,029
Parts	$36,000	35%	20%	$7,200
Administrative Cost	$23,616	0%	0% + (10%) service & parts revenue	(17,610)
TOTAL	$495,900		7%	$36,479

These totals will be used in the following section to:

1. Compare to current customer costs,
2. Determine the optimal scope of the proposal
3. Develop the appropriate proposal pricing.

Develop Profit Expectation

Customer Cost Comparison

Once you've developed a cost and profit estimate for the entire customer fleet, compare it to the current customer cost as developed in Chapter 4. Make sure to compare like costs (i.e. cost per operating hour, monthly cost, or annual cost). At this point, you must make a decision as to whether or not to pursue the deal and what cost-savings to offer the customer.

If your cost is higher than the customer's cost (as agreed upon at the end of 3), examine your cost calculations again. If you're confident in your estimates, you may decide to walk away from this contract. Another option is to change the scope of the proposal that you present. This option is discussed below.

If your cost is lower than the customer's cost, you must decide on the appropriate proposal pricing. Depending on specific conditions and characteristics of the customer, you may opt for a higher or lower profit level than the financial model amount calculated. Those options are also discussed below.

Scope of Proposal

Instead of handling every piece of equipment, you may eliminate certain segments. Use the following chart to think about how you may alter the scope:

Table 27: Determining Scope

	Cost	Risk	Profit
Unit Segment			
Service & Parts Segment			
Rental Segment			
Administrative Services			
Other Products			
Other Services			

Fill in each profit, risk, and cost box with 'high' or 'low', based on your estimates. For instance, the unit segment in our example is made up of the acquisition cost of 60 units and the training of 50 operators. There is a high cost to the unit segment, because of the acquisition cost of the units. However, the risk is low in the unit segment, because the units can be financed at a fixed rate. The profit is also low relative to the service and parts segment of the contract.

The best segments of the contract are those low in cost and risk, and high in profit. Any segments that are high in cost and risk while low in profit should be examined further and probably eliminated from the scope of the proposal. By eliminating specific high cost or high-risk segments, the price you can offer the customer should become competitive.

Appropriate Pricing

When the cost that you can offer the customer even at your financial model profit level is lower than their current cost, you have a real opportunity to sell the contract. Now you must decide the most appropriate level of pricing for this customer.

For example, the cost to the customer of your dealership managing the fleet may be calculated at $4.50 per operating hour. Current cost may be $5.75 per operating hour, as calculated in Chapter 4. If you write the proposal at $4.50 per hour, you'll be offering a 22% decrease in cost. You'll get the deal, but you also might be giving away additional profit unnecessarily. A proposal of $5.00 or $5.25 may delight the customer by offering significant savings.

On the other hand, there may be some deals that you must take at $4.75, $4.50 or even lower. Remember that in our example, the return on the Fleet Management contract was 7%. Even at 6% the contract would be more profitable than existing business in some cases. Take into consideration the following factors:

Develop A Proposal With Higher Pricing When:

- You are offering a high percentage of cost improvement
- The customer fleet has a history of perceived high quality
- You are their single source provider
- The customer has a high switching cost (due to an abundance of units, intolerance to downtime, etc.)
- This is a multi-faceted deal, where you are providing management of more than just equipment

Develop A Proposal With Lower Pricing When:

- A competitor is offering an exact match of products and services
- The customer is a target account that you've been trying to acquire for some time
- The size of the deal will make a significant impact on your company even at a lower profit level

■ The customer has a low switching cost

Once you've developed the appropriate price and scope, structure the proposal based on the benefits to the customer. Chapter 5 provides guidelines on developing the proposal.

Summary

This chapter reviewed the steps involved in determining the appropriate price to charge a customer for Fleet Management:

1. Determine the appropriate fleet mix and size to fulfill the customer's needs.

2. Develop the appropriate acquisition, usage, and administrative cost to the customer of the fleet relative to financial benchmark performance.

3. Calculate the total cost and compare it to the customer's current cost.

4. Review the scope of the proposal relative to that comparison.

5. Determine the appropriate price based on the cost findings and the specific account situation.

5. Proposal Structure - (Sales Action Plan)

Overview

This chapter lays out a suggested structure for a formal Fleet Management proposal. The proposal serves the purpose of defining in specific terms what the obligations of the dealer are in supplying Fleet Management services and what advantages those services will bring to the customer. As such it will describe cost and operational impacts with as much detail as possible in the face of incomplete information. If the customer accepts the proposal, it will serve as the basis for a formal contract. Therefore, completeness, accuracy and clarity are critical proposal elements. As a matter of procedure, the body of the proposal should be developed first, then the executive summary.

A winning proposal is the result of critical thinking based on accurate and detailed information about the customer's fleet operations. Data gathering begins with initial customer contact and will form a base for initial drafts of the proposal. It is, therefore, important for sales personnel to keep a well organized and detailed file containing information on each customer. This data organizing process should begin with a thorough search of the dealership's files including sales and maintenance records and marketing data. If the dealership has followed the preceding chapters of this book, much of this work will have been done.

As this manual indicates, preliminary cost and profitability analyses have already been done for the customer in question. These analyses will include assessments of customer costs before and after the Fleet Management implementation. Lack of specific information and uncertainty should be addressed by making reasonable assumptions about the missing data.

For the most promising customers, a draft proposal should be structured early in the process. There may be significant gaps in the proposal because of a lack of customer data. However, it is important to formally structure the information at hand in a draft proposal so that attention is drawn to the information needed. With more customer access and the attendant refined information gained through that access, each subsequent proposal draft will be better tailored for the particular customer and thus improve the chance of a win.

The remainder of this section presents an outline of a proposal with some suggestions in various parts on how to proceed. The outline is to be used as a reference not as a concrete format to which each proposal must adhere.

The Proposal Structure Outline

A. Executive Summary

This section should begin with a definition of Fleet Management as it relates to this proposal, and a review of the benefits to the customer of the agreement. Then summarize the main elements of the proposal This section should be completed following the completion of the rest of the proposal. The elements to include mirror the sections of the proposal.

1. Define Fleet Management, i.e., The dealer will:

- Identify customer Fleet Management needs
- Provide necessary equipment
- Maintain the equipment
- Administer the process

2. Review Benefits

- Expense savings per operating hour and on an annual basis
- Increased financial stability through cash infusion and elimination of fixed assets
- Increased uptime
- Ability to focus on core business

3. Proposed Fleet Mix, Costs and Pricing

- Describe the fleet determined appropriate for the account
- Review the total current cost per operating hour
- Present proposed pricing
- Summarize program savings
- List cost areas not included in the proposal

4. Program Objectives

- Strategic Objectives
- Operational Objectives

5. Proposed Solution

- Discovery
  - o Describe dealer comprehensive fleet inventory and customer operations analysis as refinement of existing customer operations knowledge base
- Fleet Buyout
  - o Give a brief description of how each category of equipment will be handled in the initial phase when/if the dealer buys the customer's equipment.
- Fleet Replacement
  - o Describe proposed replacement schedule planning process for owned and leased equipment and expected benefits

- ■ Fleet Maintenance and Repair
  - o Briefly describe the uptime goal, maintenance schedule, unexpected repair process, and guaranteed response time.
- ■ Timing and Implementation Plan
  - o List time schedule of all initial events based on time zero at contract signing

6. Future Enhancements

- ■ Include all enhancements to the program you intend to make in the future.

7. Formal Acceptance by Customer

- ■ State conditions of customer acceptance, i.e., customer issues Letter of Intent indicating acceptance and willingness to enter into contract negotiations

B. Proposed Fleet Mix, Costs, and Pricing

Use prior estimate of customer costs (Chapter 3) on the basis of available data and compare with Fleet Management pricing (Chapter 4) indicating level of savings to customer.

1. Proposed Fleet Mix

Describe the appropriate fleet size and mix as determined in Chapter 4, including rental units for peak periods and backup during unexpected repairs.

2. Current Costs

Review current total cost determined in Chapter 3 and present to the account at that point.

3. Proposal Pricing

Detail your proposed pricing structure and price level, as determined in Chapter 4.

4. Summarize Total Program Savings

Compare current cost with proposed pricing to demonstrate program savings. Consider using the chart comparing total current cost and projected cost levels to the industry average, adding a proposed pricing line.

5. Cost Areas not Included in Proposal Pricing

List all cost areas not included in the proposal and define those costs carefully. Describe the process by which they will be paid (e.g. fuel may be paid directly from the customer to a supplier; abuse charges will be billed by the dealership after repairs are completed).

C. Program Objectives

In this section list all of the customer's objectives in implementing the program. You've segmented the objectives into Strategic and Operational to address the objectives of all levels of management at the customer account. Below you list possible objectives to include.

1. Strategic Objectives

- Assure customer satisfaction on all fronts
- Eliminate cost of owning fleet
- Reduce cost of operating fleet
- Modernize fleet through judicious replacement schedule
- Improve customer's balance sheet by removing fleet assets and associated liabilities
  - o Improve ROA and ROE
  - o Increase debt capacity
- Properly size fleet(s)
- Increase flexibility

- Provide management reporting to reduce waste and improve efficiency
- Reduce customer's administrative staff and costs by removing the total Fleet Management burden
- Hold operating facilities accountable for supporting the contractor's (dealer's) efforts
- Encourage responsible operational practices
- Exceed contract economic targets

2. Operational Objectives

- Superior fleet availability
- Modern, productive, and safe fleet
- Compliance with OSHA standards
- Total operator satisfaction
- Proper equipment configuration vis-à-vis operational requirements
- Eliminate capital appropriation process for fleet equipment
- Single supplier of fleet services
- Sensitive and proactive to customers' fleet needs

D. Proposed Solution

Describe in this section the post-contract dealer actions and various phases of the implementation. Make sure it is clearly stated that these actions are to be taken after a formal contract is signed. Emphasize that following acquisition or conversion of all customer-owned units the dealer will have put customer's entire fleet into a monthly contract with centralized billing.

1. Discovery

Identify areas needing further analysis on case specific basis - level of effort depends on closeness of customer contact during data gathering and synthesis in 3.0 and 4.0.

Comprehensive inventory of fleet including:

- Brand

- Model
- Manufacture Date
- Serial #
- Meter hours
- Book Value
- Application
- Lessor and lease terms (if applicable)

2. Dealer Buyout of Customer Fleet

Owned Equipment - Refer to Chapter 6 for a methodology to determine appropriate buyout price. In this section state the methodology you propose to determine value. The contract will contain the actual buyout figures.

- Equipment less than 5 years old
- Equipment over 5 years old
- Equipment Designated "Immediate Replacement" (Serviced on "time & materials" basis until replaced or eliminated)

Parts Repurchase - State the methodology by which you will assume ownership of the parts inventory, such as:

- Dealer buys back your brand parts based on a schedule to be determined less a 20% restocking charge.
- Competitive brand parts will be inventoried and priced based on aftermarket demand/scrap value.
- Leased Units - Dealer will, where feasible, buy out, assume, or administer existing leases.

Lease buy out units will be treated as formerly owned units as above.

- Assumed or administered leases will be treated as buy out units for pricing purposes

3. Fleet Replacement

Describe the proposal short term replacement schedule and long term replacement program including:

- Establishing model standardization whenever possible
- Replacing all units with your brand units to maximize efficiency (Monthly rental fee for new units always less than or equal to the units being replaced)

4. Fleet Maintenance and Repair

Describe the proposed maintenance program including:

- Scheduled maintenance
- Response time standards for spot maintenance
- Other constraints (e.g., service during customer's normal working hours)
- Availability and loaner terms
- Abuse definitions and billings
- Specify weekend and evening coverage
- Specify maintenance management system for breakdowns and data tracking including:
  - Management reports to customer on service leading to corrective action
  - Customer contacts and responsibilities for data tracking
  - Breakdown checklist including
    - Type of breakdown
    - Model/serial #
    - Time of call
    - Time technician arrives
    - Service quality
    - Date & time of second visit if necessary
    - Date & time unit is operational
- Abuse Reduction Program including
  - Dealer actions to eliminate equipment abuse costs including
  - Establishment of baseline abuse costs for each customer site
  - Recommendations for the right operator training and management actions to achieve baseline abuse costs

5. Timing and Implementation Plan

Insert a proposed schedule for the implementation of the proposed solution.

E. Future Enhancements

This section should include all enhancements to the program you intend to make in the future, if applicable. Suggestions are listed below.

1. Product Technology

■ Your brand is a leader in equipment management.

2. Employ Communications Technology

■ Dealers, following the manufacturer's lead, will use latest electronic communications to rapidly exchange data (i.e., key pads and computerized vehicle tracking equipment).

3. Inclusion of Other Customer Equipment

■ For example:
  o Sweepers
  o Personnel Carriers
  o Scissors Lifts
  o Cranes
  o Skid Steers
  o Water Trucks
  o Dump Trucks

4. Customer Layout and Instillation Consulting

F. Formal Acceptance

This section should outline the steps involved in progressing to a Fleet Management contract agreement.

1. Letter of Intent (LOI)

Upon receiving an LOI from the customer dealer will take preliminary action while a formal contract is negotiated.

This preliminary action includes specifying dealer personnel who will play key roles in the project.

2. Execute Formal Contract

3. Specify Project Launch Team

Comprised of key personnel from dealer and customer

Structure and review implementation plan including performance benchmarks.

4. Dealer and Customer Jointly Announce the Project

Summary

This chapter reviewed the components of a standard proposal. The proposal should be developed during the course of the customer analysis and pricing process. Upon completion, it should be presented to the customer as a basis for discussion and negotiation. The goal of the proposal is to present all facets of the program leading to continually more definition and finally a formal Fleet Management contract.

6. Initial Activities - (Performing to Contract)

Overview

Congratulations! You've won the contract and in order to make money, you now need to execute it flawlessly to make money. This chapter and the next talk about the issues you will be managing to make this happen. There are two primary breakdowns of this end of the business. First, there are the Initial Events. These are the activities you need to do immediately, such as handling the transition of ownership for the equipment and possibly the parts. Also, you will need to do an initial service to the equipment, bringing it up to your standards of quality running condition. You will cover these initial activities in six different areas:

- Repurchase
- Re-Rent or Stand-By-Equipment
- Staffing
- Initial Service of the Equipment
- Training Operators
- Training Dealership Employees

The next chapter covers the On-Going Functions, or what you deal with everyday of the contract.

Repurchase

Generally there are two areas that you will be involved in "re-purchasing" when you enter into a Fleet Management contract; they are repurchasing the equipment the customer already owns and the parts that might be in their maintenance inventory.

Equipment

There are basically four steps in repurchasing the equipment:

- Identify all equipment.
- Establish the value of each piece of equipment.
- Complete the paperwork that gives you ownership of the equipment.
- Handle the payment to the customer for the equipment and parts.

Remember, in this transaction, although you now own the equipment, it stays where it is until you begin the equipment replacement process. You will discuss that process in the next chapter.

Identifying the Equipment

It may seem obvious, but both you and the customer need a very clear and detailed inventory of the equipment. You are going to be buying it, and the customer is going to be selling. Each of you wants a good deal and no deal is good that doesn't meet the needs of both parties. Accuracy is very important in this step. Some of the details you might consider including in your inventory of the equipment are listed in the first table. The second table is used if there is financing still in effect for any of this equipment.

Table 28: Equipment Inventory Identification

Field	Individual Detail
Make	
Model	
Mfg. Year	
Serial Number	
Condition	
Attachments (not otherwise itemized)	
Current Owner	
Comments	

If there is a financing company involved with any units or equipment, then you will also need to include material similar to the fields shown below for each unit. It is possible that based on the expiration of the equipment loan you might consider replacing it either early or late in the replacement cycle.

Table 29: Financed Equipment Details

Field	Individual Detail
Finance Company	
Loan Balance	
Interest Rate	
Monthly Payment	
Loan Termination Date	
Comments	

Establishing Value of the Equipment

How do you determine the value of the equipment? There are a number of ways. Some of the ones for you to consider are:

- Book value
- Wholesale value
- Loan value
- Outside appraisal

The condition of the equipment may have a bearing on the value of the equipment. Consider using the manufacturer's inspection form to establish equipment condition. This is standardized and the customer will understand the thoroughness that you have invested into evaluating the equipment.

Who is responsible for valuation? As the buyer you will want to be the primary contact for the valuation, but you might find customers who insist on being involved. One of the important issues here is that you keep track of who is doing it, when it is getting done, and that the values are reasonable. You are taking possession of this equipment and these values will be on you books. Although some of the "influencers" or "resources" for reconciliation points are listed, using the customer as the primary source or control for establishing valuation is not recommended. Some of the possible options are:

Dealer Sales Department

- Dealer Accounting Department
- Customer Purchasing Department
- Customer Accounting Department
- All of the above

Change In Ownership

When you take possession of the equipment you should have a specific list of what documentation you need, who has to sign it, if it needs to be recorded or filed and what detailed copies the customer is going to get.

- Title for equipment
- Leasing documents
- Who handles the paperwork?

Payment

How you structure the transaction may be unique in each case, but you will of course want to take a number of issues into account. What are your plans for the cash flow, payment in check, credit against subsequent billing, funding through dealership, vendor, leasing company, or third party organization?

Consider also the impact on the balance sheet. (Are you structured in such a way that this will not damage the asset and lending balance? What does it do to your debt to equity, etc.?)

Consider creating a checklist, which you first go over with the people in your dealership. Be sure to review the Fleet Management contracts for any special or unique issues. You might want to review this checklist with the customer before the transaction takes place so that there are no surprises. Don't short cut. Go through the entire checklist and do everything in sequence as you have it itemized.

Parts Inventory

The second category of assets frequently repurchased, as part of a Fleet Management contract, is the maintenance parts inventory. You've already signed the contract. Now you need to understand the process of establishing the value for these parts, acquiring them and putting them on your books.

Steps in Repurchasing Parts Inventory

Creating An Inventory

- Generate an inventory of all parts. Frequently customers have acquired parts over a long period of time and their inventory is in bad shape.
- Some of the possible options to consider when you are planning an inventory or repurchase are:
    - What is the size of the parts inventory involved?
    - Who has been providing the parts in the past?
    - Should you take a "Full Detailed Inventory"?
    - Or should you do a "Spot Inventory"?

Group the parts by brand or agreed-on category - several of the category methods are illustrated below in 2 charts:

Table 30: Grouping Parts by Age

Age of Parts	Credit Allowed
Less than 12 months old	100%
More than 12 months old	60%
Obsolete	On Consignment

Table 31: Grouping Parts by Brand

Brand	Credit Allowed
Your Brand	See Chart Above
Your Replacement Compatible	See Chart Above
Other Brand	On Consignment

Identify retail price for each part (if appropriate) and any discount or markdown agreed upon.

You need to have a clean method of establishing the price on these parts. Frequently you will either not take all parts, or not give full value for all parts. There are many ways to do this:

- Customer's asset value or last purchase price, as determined by their invoices or inventory system
- Your retail parts price lists less certain discounts as illustrated in the charts above
- Contingency price if you can use or sell the parts acquired
- Scrap value if the customer chooses not to keep the parts
- Outside wholesaler or will-fit vendor's pricing or evaluation
- Total by category and for the entire inventory
- Present to customer and get signature
- Receiving Parts into your company

Once all prices have been agreed upon and valuation signed by the customer, either package and move parts to your location or leave them at the customer's location for your use in this contract.

These parts are generally available in your dealership for any equipment repairs that occur. They usually are not allocated solely to this customer's units. Your people need to be told this. Part of the idea here is to improve the inventory performance, both yours and the customers. You've taken care of theirs already, now what can you do about yours?

Accounting for Parts

If they are being moved to your location, you should have created a purchase order for them. Receive them as you would any other merchandise and assign a value to each item in your inventory.

If they are being received at less than the new part's value because you negotiated a good deal, then be sure to book the appropriate lower inventory value for the difference. If you allowed more credit than they were worth, then be sure to book the appropriate expense.

Plans for Parts Disposition

Some of these parts you repurchased have little value to you. What are you going to do about them once you receive them? Some options to consider are:

Negotiate a parts return for your brand parts with your manufacturer's representative. Even if you take a charge for return, they may be worth more to you this way than leaving them on the shelf, inactive.

For competitive brand parts or obsolete parts of your own brand that neither you nor manufacturer has any use for, consider advertising them through the Internet.

If, in the process of taking over a fleet, you have parts for other brands of equipment, contact a dealer of that brand and negotiate a return of these parts, if they are not going to be needed in the ongoing service of these units.

Procedures If the Parts Are Maintained at the Customer Site
- Inventory of parts in the customer's maintenance area
- Procedure for using or removing parts from remote inventory
- Procedure for updating or replacing inventory
- Periodic check of inventory levels and accuracy

Re-Rent (Equipment)

You now need to set up the equipment in your billing system to generate invoices at the appropriate frequency (monthly, weekly, quarterly) and for the appropriate units of measure. For example, certain items might be billed at the number of hours run or at a flat monthly charge. You should already have the specified method and price for each unit based on the work you did back in Chapter 4, "Developing Pricing." If you need to discuss any changes, they will probably have to be internal, since you already have a contract.

Staffing

In each contract you need to assess your capacity and the financial benchmarks related to personnel expense. Each department needs to be involved. You have grouped cost categories into three areas: acquisition, usage and administration. You'll follow the same grouping here.

Acquisition Staff Requirements

Purchasing

This function will be part of the existing sales department because the needs are known from year to year with more accuracy and forewarning. Getting the right equipment delivered on time should be easier. It is not expected that you will need additional staff because of a particular contract. If you look at the guidelines for the number of overhead people in the sales department, you will find usually a 3:1 ratio of sales people to administrators. This also translates to about one sales coordinator for every $750,000 of annual gross profit. Therefore, when your Fleet Management contracts begin to total $750,000 GP annually for the units alone, you should consider a dedicated purchaser.

Equipment Usage Staffing

Equipment

Unless you are supplying operators, the only staffing requirements you'll have related to units are operator trainers. Review the section in this chapter entitled Training Operators before determining trainer needs.

Service Department

How many technicians are needed? How large is the contract for Fleet Management?

You generally find for light equipment you will need one technician for 100 to 125 units when dealing with a single shift operation and medium to light duty usage. Other applications and conditions, such as heavier equipment where general maintenance runs 30-40 hours a year for each unit, will require adaptation and fewer equipment expectations per technician.

Are they assigned or allocated to the contract?

You might dedicate technicians or you might include technicians as they are available. You will need to consider their scheduling and the contract commitments when making this decision.

Annual Income from 60 Units

Category	Sales	Rental	Service	Parts	FM Coordination	G&A	Total	Annual Figures Per Unit
Sales	248,400		150,660	36,000	24,436		459,496	7,658.27
COGS	211,140		52,731	25,200			289,071	4,817.85
GP	37,260		97,929	12,600	24,436		172,225	2,870.42
Personnel	18,630		30,132	3,600		9,333	86,131	1,435.52
								Per Unit

Table 32: Personnel Expense Calculation

The level of other service staff such as service manager, PM scheduler, dispatcher, etc. is generally guided by a couple of benchmarks. The first is a benchmark of at least 5 technicians for every overhead person. The second benchmark is the financial model. Based on the procedures you used in Chapter 4 for Developing Pricing on an example of a 60 unit fleet your annual income by department will look like the chart previously.

Note: the personnel expense allocated to service is based on model performance. That expense level should cover the benefits related to the technicians' wages and all other service staff.

Parts Department

How many parts people are needed for this size contract?

Since you all understand that pricing on the contract was done at retail price, you should be able to determine the number of people needed to handle the parts side of the contract by looking at the amount of parts expected in this contract.

A parts person should be handling $50,000 in retail sales volume per month or $600,000 annually. Compare that figure with the parts consumption expected.

Table 33: Calculation of Number of Parts Staff Based on Annual Contract Parts Consumption

Annual Parts Consumption Per Unit		Number of Units In Contract		Annual Parts Volume
$ 1,200	X	125	=	$ 150,000
Monthly Employee Sales Volume		Number of Months		Annual Sales Volume Handled by One Parts Employee
$ 50,000	X	12	=	$ 600,000

Obviously in this illustration you only need one-quarter of one person's time to handle the parts involved with this contract.

It is also possible that you have been handling the parts for this customer prior to the contract. In that case you might not see a need for additional parts people because you are merely shifting the parts business from the customer directly to the customer through the contract.

Administrative Staffing Needs

Is there a contract administrator?

Generally handling a Fleet Management contract is similar to handling the service department. There is the need for one overhead staff position for every five or more technicians. In this single contract you may not have enough volume to require a fully dedicated contract administrator. Eventually you might have enough units under contract to justify this dedicated person.

While this example may not match the fleet or contract pricing you are using, it can be used as a method of reviewing the staffing needs and expense allocation relative to a new contract.

Initial Service (PM) on Equipment

Part of any good contract will include an agreement that you perform an initial inspection and maintenance of the equipment, and thereby bring it up to good quality performance standards. In handling this function at the beginning of the contract you should identify certain details:

- Use the _____ Point Inspection Form
- It should be performed with in the first ___ days following the beginning of the contract.
- The customer is responsible for the PM billing for the initial work Yes ☐ No ☐
- This initial PM or Inspection is expected to take ___ hours per unit.
- Equipment repair/service write up will be done on the manufacturer's inspection form.
- With the write up from the inspection _____ will visit the customer by the end of the 1st quarter of the contract to explain new procedures and how billing and reporting will be handled during the contract.

Use this as a checklist of functions so that you make sure all activities are taken care of.

Training Operations

Driver Training

Training has been shown to have a significant impact on the abuse cost and general repair cost of equipment. It is recommended that this be treated as a major issue with the customer and that your trainer be scheduled to work with the customer's operators very early in the contract and on a regular basis.

Plan the Training Location This might be done at the dealership as a dedicated training class for the customer or with other people who are participating in your training programs. Or, it might be done at the customer location with their equipment and dedicated to their people alone.

Choosing the Instructor Do you have a dedicated trainer? You might consider a trainer from the service or sales department for this project if you don't have a dedicated trainer. Be sure to review the material in the manufacturer's Operator Training Course and consider what impact the operator's performance has on the profitability of the contract.

Good Size for a Class Ideal classes are those that allow the operator the required time on the machine they are being trained to run and enough time to come back and review areas that they find difficult. Keep in mind that if the equipment you are placing in the customer's site for this contract is new to the operators that you will want to include more time than if you are continuing with the existing equipment.

Use the Manufacturer's Operator Training Course There are other training courses and you can create your own, but why would you want to spend time re-inventing what already exists?

Schedule of Training

- Initial Training (Plan this with the customer, and possibly include it in the contract schedule.)
- Plan refresher courses for drivers of equipment demonstrating high abuse billing.
- Schedule annual or regular courses of follow up of driver training.

Use a computer program to track who has been trained, what their scores were, and what material was in their course. This is very similar to tracking the calls a salesperson makes to the customers. For some dealers this might be done in a unique part of your sales call tracking software.

Recognition For Operators Who Have A Good Record

Employees strive for recognition. This is true whether they are your employees or your customer's employees. Consider awarding the operators certificates for safe, efficient and abuse-free operation of the equipment.

Consider posting a "Good Operator" Scoreboard.

Training Dealership Employees

The conditions of a Fleet Management contract change the approach of the service that is performed. In many dealerships this is the first time that the equipment being serviced is not owned by the customer. In this respect it is very similar to the rental department service conditions. Because of this, you should have an agreement about the level of service work to be performed, the cost involved and the interval between PM services.

Ownership Responsibilities

The dealership owns this equipment. You want your equipment serviced well.

PM Schedule

Regular testing will tell you what a good frequency for PM should be. Based on how you quoted this contract, previous experience with this equipment and new oils and maintenance options you may want PM work done more frequently or less frequently than you do with traditional customers.

Selection of Parts

The primary concern is for the service quality of the repair and the parts involved. You lose money if you have to go back and service equipment for the same problem a second time. Rework is not beneficial to our customer or us. It costs us money and the customer experiences down time. Therefore, plan on using quality parts. They are not expensive; they are a good investment.

Your brand parts are always the preferred choice.

When your brand parts can't be used, expect that you will check compatibility through the compatibility parts program, which can fit much of the service needs for competitive brand equipment.

When these first two options don't adequately solve your needs, then expect your best option is OEM brand parts for the particular equipment being serviced.

Other options may be utilized if you have exhausted the three options already listed.

Your parts department staff is probably very experienced in sourcing parts for other brands of equipment.

Identification of Repair Needs

The process of finding the extra work when performing an PM service is sometimes interpreted by technicians as a negative consequence of doing inspections. The reverse is true. The cost of having to come back and perform service when it breaks is more expensive for us as a dealership and creates downtime for the customer. This is a contract you have committed to.

- Is the PM schedule correct? Should it be longer or shorter?
- What additional work needs to be performed now?
- What service work needs to be scheduled for follow-up?
- What is the overall condition? Is there a trend that you should consider dealing with in some fashion?
- Is there abuse that needs to be taken care of?
- What recommendations can you make to improve the performance or servicing of this equipment?

Involve the technicians in these analyses. They see the equipment every day. They also know the working conditions of the equipment.

Summary

This chapter attempted to cover the points you will need to deal with as you take over the operation of a new Fleet Management contract. Keep in mind that this is possibly one of many contracts. You need to keep a big picture vision while doing very detailed and accurate work.

Keep everyone constantly reminded that this is a new contract for the customer and you are dealing with procedures that the customer employees may not have had to deal with before. Explain steps to the customer and internal employees as you go through them.

In addition, use the checklists mentioned in this chapter so that you continue to follow procedures and cover all details. This is a sign of professionalism to the customer.

It is time to go on to the "on-going" functions of every-day activity.

- Repurchase
- Re-Rent or Stand-By-Equipment
- Staffing
- Initial Service of the Equipment
- Training Operators
- Training Dealership Personnel

7. Ongoing Functions - (Performing to Contract)

Overview

This section will investigate the daily functions of supplying and servicing the equipment, performing efficient PM service, and what happens if you can't place the equipment back in service immediately. Again the focus is on the operation, the acquisition of equipment, the usage or maintenance functions, and the administration of the process. A large amount of this chapter will be administration, talking about the monitoring and reporting of profitability, response time and uptime. Each of these sections will be broken down to more specific and manageable pieces.

Equipment Replacement Cycle

In Fleet Management Contracts, dealers generally commit to a replacement cycle on the equipment. This keeps the age of the units low and the uptime high. There are two basic areas: planning when and what units get replaced and then what to do with the units you are retiring from the customer's site.

What Equipment To Retire

The first units to consider for replacement are those that create consistent "unscheduled downtime" - this is when the unit is down during the customer's production time. If units can be serviced during the customer's non-productive time (2nd shift, etc.). then even higher maintenance may be tolerated, but the contract commitment to the customer is that they will experience higher levels of production as a result of you handling their equipment. That has to be the prime directive.

Cycling the units is part of your plan. Whatever the ownership alternatives, you are looking to continuously infuse the contract with your brand of equipment and retire, replace and eliminate any other brand equipment. You should have a program designed to replace older or competitive equipment. This might be done through a chart similar to the following:

Table 34: Estimate of Equipment Cycle Program

Years	Eq 1	Eq 2	Eq 3	Total
Yr 1	20.00%	40.00%	20.00%	22.86%
Yr 2	20.00%	30.00%	20.00%	21.43%
Yr 3	20.00%	20.00%	20.00%	20.00%
Yr 4	20.00%	10.00%	20.00%	18.57%
Yr 5	20.00%		20.00%	17.14%
	100.00%	100.00%	100.00%	100.00%

- *Planned replacement schedule; of course the total percentages will change with the mix of units and the speed you plan for replacement*

There may be a variety of different replacement cycles based on different criteria. Some of the possible criteria to consider are the age of the equipment, the brands of equipment, and the experience level of your staff to service certain brands or models. Your ability to get or develop training for servicing equipment could also play into your decision of what equipment is covered or cycled quickly out of the fleet.

The two graphs below are a method of looking at some of this issue. In the first graph the concern would be if the number of hours a unit is down as a percentage of the hours the customer is operating similar equipment, then you should be concerned about getting that unit replaced as early as possible. Review the conditions of the unit to see if it is abuse or the wrong application for that equipment. Operator training talked about in the last chapter might be a solution.

The second graph below shows the steady increase of maintenance cost over a number of months. If this is predictable and expected, you're in great shape. If the slope of that line is very steep or rising faster than expected, then you should investigate that unit or group of units for possible replacement. Equipment which qualifies in this category, might also qualify in the first problem, but this is not always the case.

Table 35: Unit Replacement Criteria

Purchase Cycle Of New Equipment

If you have a planned replacement cycle in the contract you should have the purchasing for these units in your annual purchasing plan. You want to be sure that you have enough lead-time planned that they not only arrive in time but you can have them prepped and schedule their delivery without having to utilize overtime, rush deliveries, or outside delivery services, if possible. The disposal of equipment being replaced was discussed above.

Below is a sample form for tracking new purchases relative to the Fleet Management contract. The expectation here is that you will have advance notice of the needs and be buying well ahead of the needed delivery to the customer. As you know some times, you will juggle the actual units and delivery schedule to meet specific customer needs. Hopefully, this form will help you in that area.

Table 36: New Equipment Purchasing Control Sheet

Units to Buy & Model	Quantity & Confirmation #	Date Needed	Date Ordered	Date Last Verified

Of course when you planned the contract, you planned the issues of balancing your assets and liabilities. But, have you discussed the financing arrangements with your banker, your leasing company, your major vendors, etc?

What To Do With The Units Coming Off The Contract

Keeping in mind that you choose what units are replaced, or cycled out of the fleet, you should have published a listing of these units to your sales people. Include all relevant information, such as make, model, year of manufacture, condition, retail price and dates the equipment will be available. You might consider offering these units at a slight discount if they are sold before the date available or offering a better commission to the sales people during this time.

Table 37: Sample Sheet of Equipment Availability for Salesperson to Pre-Sell Equipment

Serial #	Description	Date Available	Selling Price	Make	Model	Condition

Possible options for units coming out of a fleet arrangement are:

- Have the unit "pre-sold" before it becomes available
- Use the unit in your rental fleet
- Wholesale Sales

Service

PM Scheduling

One of the first areas to plan for regular functions is the PM scheduling. Since this is now your equipment, you want the best and more efficient service for the equipment. This does not mean over-servicing the equipment but it also is not under-servicing it. There is a correct balance for this equipment.

Frequency

While there have been frequencies in place for years, many dealers have recently found they have been doing too much service on units. With the advent of synthetic oils, better testing technology and computer systems to track the effects of PM service, you will find that the cycle can be extended.

Ways to Maximize the Schedule

In order to make money with a Fleet Management contract you will need to monitor your PM activity closely. Part of this is watching the hours invested in PM and the other is watching the dollars. There are various ways to keep these costs and dollars down. Some of them are listed below:

- Planning all PM service that needs to be done in the next XX days or weeks and sending the appropriate number of technicians to do the service in one day, or half of a day, etc. Make sure that a technician investing travel time is spending the entire day at the customer site, either conducting necessary PM's or performing repairs.
- Being sure that all parts are on hand and in possession of the technician who is going to perform the PM
- Monitoring the time taken by technicians for a PM
- Monitoring return trips for repair after PM work
- Expecting in terms of average time per PM

You should be very clear with your technicians about what is included and not included in a PM service. This should be on a printed work-order that they use when doing the service and they should follow the checklist.

If they identify additional work to be done on a particular unit, they should call back to the dispatcher and discuss the work. In consultation with the dispatcher or service manager, they then evaluate the needs and the time involved. In some cases the dealership (represented by these three people) will choose to repair the unit right then, repair it later, send another technician, or substitute it with a rental unit.

Reporting Information for PM

Because scheduling PM Service is conditional on the number of hours between service you need to track certain pieces of information. Listed below is the information needed to track profitability, technician productivity, and accumulated cost per unit.

- Hours between service
- Parts Dollars used
- Labor Dollars used
- Labor Hours Used
- Travel Time and/or mileage
- Additional Service Work Performed
- Identification of parts needed for regular PM activity

You should expect very good fill rates on PM parts. Your needs are known in advance, and you have time to be sure that all parts are at the dealership or the customer site before you actually assign the technician. Below is a short checklist to work with:

- When planning PM work all parts are generally known.
- Parts should be ordered early enough as to be available in time
- A "Parts Needed for PM Service" report should be used and reviewed by the service department and then submitted as a parts request to the parts department.
- All parts should be in a database by serial number for scheduling and purchasing.

Table 38: Parts Needs for PM Repairs

Part #	Description	Quantity	Unit #	PM Due Date	Vendor	Delivery Date

The report illustrated may also be sorted by vendor for purchasing, by customer or location for assembling the parts, and for distribution to the technicians.

Repair and Dispatching

No matter how good your PM activities are, equipment breaks down. Metal wears, oil and grease accumulate and operators don't pay the attention that they should. You will need to do repairs. To keep costs to a minimum and customer satisfaction high, consider the following actions.

Define Priorities

Be clear, be proactive and communicate your priorities with everyone involved. This might be an internal issue, or it might involve the customer. What constitutes an emergency? If a seat is torn, or a back-up alarm is not functioning, is that the same as a smoking engine or slipping brakes? Not only do you need to define the importance, but you also should consider defining the response time for different issues.

Table 39: Repair Priority Sheet

Issue	Response Time	Priority / Importance	Field or Shop
Broken Light			
Smoking Engine			
Slipping brakes			

Part of the issue here is not merely responding to the customer, but also establishing quality levels and expectations that the customer can rely on. You want to deliver quality to the customer, but you also want the customer to know that when they call they will get the same good service and answer from who ever takes the call.

Create A Procedure For The Customer To Contact You

One of the most important issues for a customer experiencing a problem is being able to reach someone and knowing what to do to get service. You need to have a clear procedure.

A major part of the Fleet Management function is your commitment to relieving the customer of troubles and assisting them in focusing on their core business. One of the top rated issues today in handling service is the customer's difficulty in reaching the supplier for service.

Although simplicity would direct you to assign one person at the customer's site as the contact person, customers do not want to get into a bottle neck. Yet it is almost impossible to allow "anyone" to call for service. You will need to evaluate the customer's organization and equipment management needs. Based on these issues you will want to design the most efficient program for handling service needs for the customer and you.

One way of helping the customer when they need to contact you is to attach a label or decal to every piece of equipment explaining how they can contact you and identifying the steps for them to take. Also consider a toll-free number if the scope of the contract locations makes it necessary to use long distance telephone calls. Illustrated below is a sample label.

Table 40: Customer Label for Reporting Breakdowns

Please use the following steps when requesting service for this equipment. ■ Call _____ (800) xxx-xxxx (24 hrs / 365 days a year). ■ Please have the following information ready when you call:	■ Company Name ■ Department Identification (or job site) ■ Equipment Unit Number (found stenciled on the _____) ■ Hour Meter Reading (found ......)

It might be advisable for you to provide to the customer a series of ways to contact you for help and service such as the following group of phone numbers.

- Dealership Phone Number
- Service Department Direct Phone Number
- Night Time Phone Number
- Service Manager's Home Phone Number (or Cellular Number)
- Dealer Principal's Home Number (or Cellular Number)
- Technician's Home Phone Number (or Cellular Number)

On a regular basis, you might want to communicate with the customer to be sure that they feel they have enough access to you for assistance.

Train Staff on Procedures

Create a system for your service staff for responding to the customer call, and train your employees. Clarify any uncertainty with technicians, dispatchers, other departments, customers, and even other sub-contractors. Resolve any conditional issues by identifying what the alternatives might be. The issues to cover are:

- Who may be contacted by the customer
- How they should use the priority list to schedule the repair
- Who should report the repair schedule to the customer
- Who should dispatch the technician
- When should they employ a replacement unit
- What internal reporting must be completed

Abuse Repair

Definition of Abuse and Repair Procedure

The definition of abuse for each contract should already be established.

- Any repair the technician believes is not included in the contract should be discussed with the correct people back at the dealership before that person confronts the customer.
- It may be necessary to have the customer sign that abuse repair was performed. You will improve the implementation of this if you have first discussed it between technician and dispatcher, or service manager before talking to the customer about it.
- Have an explanation of what caused the abuse, how it can be avoided and what steps you recommend for the customer so that it will not happen again.

Billing Abuse

- Don't delay abuse billing
- Explain the circumstances of what the abuse was, what caused it, what options exist for assuring that it doesn't happen again
- Review all abuse billings with the customer regularly

Reporting Abuse Service

Summarize abuse billings by:

- Location
- Shift Operation
- Model
- Usage or Attachments

Use these reports for analysis to explain to the customer and the operators what causes abuse. It is imperative that you keep the abuse billing down. These units are your equipment, and the customer is not expecting to pay any more than you have in the contract. See the section on driver training and recognition of good driving and operations for more suggestions on controlling this expense.

Parts Management

Inventory Investment in Parts

Using the methods described in Chapter 4, you should already have estimated the parts consumption per unit per year. In addition, now that a PM schedule has been established and initial maintenance on the units has been done, much of the inventory needs can be identified. Use the parts dollar consumption estimate and your average parts turnover rate to calculate your average inventory investment.

Equation 1: Calculation of Inventory Investment Based on Contract Parts Consumption

Parts Sales $	X	COGS %	=	COGS $ Value
	X		=	
COGS $ Value	+	Inventory Turnover Rate	=	Average Inventory Investment
	+		=	

What Is The Method Of Keeping The Right Mix Of Parts?

One method of assuring a good fill rate of parts for the equipment covered in the contract is to cross reference the various models through a function of what primary parts are needed in their service. These might be parts for PM and expected general repairs.

You might be able to use previous history on some equipment or models to determine what parts are used most frequently.

On some newer models you will need to extrapolate from your experience with similar models what group of parts should be considered for stocking.

You might want to group these parts into three groups for planning:

- PM
- Repairs under 4 hours
- Repairs over 4 hours

This list developed of service parts should be cross-referenced with what parts are actually stocking parts. Care should be taken for parts that qualified but are not "stocking parts."

Table 41: Identification of Parts Carried by Dealership

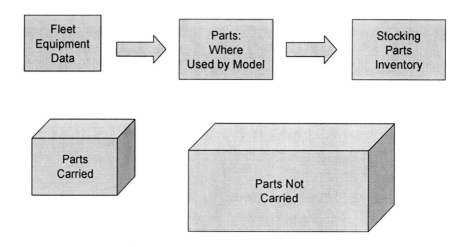

The diagram above shows a simple process whereby the details of the fleet are checked for all parts that will/would be needed to repair the fleet of equipment. This list of all possible parts is compared to the stocking parts inventory. From this list you then get two groups of parts: first, the list of parts that you already stock; second, the list of parts to consider carrying.

In the first list, you might want to look at the depth of stock relative to the new units in the fleet.

In the second list, you probably want to consider carrying more of these parts than previously stocked. Usually equipment dealers carry parts based on service history of breakdowns. One major difference here is you're looking for zero downtime. In order to accomplish this, you have to carry more parts than before. But, you know the history of the service for these units; you know the PM schedule, the fact that you are the sole supplier for service and the number of units under contract. You should be able to do a better job of this with all of this information.

You may want to have a discussion about the frequency of repair using certain parts, based on the age of various units before that repair happens the number of units being covered and the probability of need. Off-setting these issues will be the severity of the repair or downtime based on not having a certain part or group of parts.

Parts experience a certain life cycle. There is a point at which you will find heavy repairs and then the amount of parts needed will decline significantly. In some cases this will begin about the end of the second year, peak in the fourth year and begin to level off or decline after that point.

Expectations for The Parts Department

You should consider establishing clear expectations for each department, and this department is no different than the rest. What is the definition of good management here? Generally it is fill rate, turnover, profitability and productivity. Establish for the contract as well as the department in general what the expectations of performance are:

Parts Turnover   _____ X

Parts Staffing $_____ / Month / Employee

Parts Fill Rate   _____ %

Parts Gross Profit   _____ %

These four items above begin to establish the benchmarks for a parts department. If you can attain all four you are running a good parts department.

Rental

Some customers have peak seasons during which they need additional units. If you looked at all of the aspects of the customer and planned this in the contract, it still needs to be monitored. The charge for the rental units should be against the contract. There are also times when you decide not to repair a unit on-site or immediately. In these cases you want to replace the down unit with a short-term rental unit. This replacement unit should be charged against the contract and specifically the down unit. Below are listed some areas to discuss and plan for before they happen.

- Repair
- Mix of equipment available for the contract
- When to use rental equipment vs. repairing, or while repairing
- Peak Period Scheduling
- Procedure for delivering unit
- Procedure for removing unit
- Rental Check In/Check Out

Administrative

After signing any Fleet Management contract good practices would be to return to the dealership and call a meeting of all people who will be involved with the customer or involved with the contract administration. Some of these people might be:

- Dealer Principal
- Rental Manager
- Sales Manager
- Technician(S)
- Service Manager
- Dispatcher
- Parts Manager
- Billing Clerk(s)

- Site Supervisors
- Aftermarket Sales People

- Marketing Coordinator
- Others

Covering expectations of the customer, the scope of the contract, the locations of the customer's fleet, the billing process, etc. will be time consuming but beneficial if it makes the management of this fleet successful. Starting out you might want to have a check list of issues to be discussed. Use this book as a starting point for discussion ideas. Eventually you will have enough experience with contracts that you will all come with your own checklist for discussion points.

Schedule regular review meetings of these people to go over the contract and your progress. If you are measuring yourself against the estimate and you're not beating the estimate you need to take some internal measures. You should certainly be measuring performance against the financial benchmarks as well. Each contract should be reviewed at least quarterly.

In this section you are going to group the discussion of administrative work into four main areas:

1. The **External Billing Process** will cover Single and Multiple Location Account, Control Number, Term and Timing, and Overtime

2. The **Internal Billing Process** is about tracking your cost once the customer revenue has been posted.

3. **Monitoring & Dealer Reports** discusses the analysis of profitability, technician productivity, abuse indicators and warranty recovery.

4. **Contract Performance** covers those reports that would assist the customer in visualizing your success in han-

dling the contract. Review reports such as Response Time, Equipment Downtime and the Guaranteed Savings Report.

The External Billing Process

The billing functions for Fleet Management break down into a couple of areas. Those that go to the customer you will deal with here, and will be referred to as external billing, or billing that goes outside the company.

Multiple Income Locations

One style of billing for Fleet Management is to have all elements of the bill segregated in the background, and posted to the various departments income accounts. In this style the customer gets one price for the 'unit of billing' or measure. This could be a monthly bill, or bill for XX number of hours in a month. But internally you have an income posted for labor, parts, travel, fuel, rental and even administration of the Fleet Management function. Then all expenses and cost of operation get posted the way that they always have.

Single Income Center

A second option used in some companies its to post income to one central cost center and then charge all related expenses to that 'department'. In this condition you have the same single invoice to the customer and NO itemized breakdown of the income to various departments. But as the charges occur for labor, purchasing parts, travel expenses, etc., they are all posted to this department. Sometimes this causes confusion of how much of some expenses to post to this department. Other situations are confusing in areas such as labor utilization, total travel expense for vehicles, company response time, etc. Whatever the decision you should consider the positive and negative consequences to your choices.

Terms and Timing of Billing

If you are going to bill the customer monthly and invoices are due in ten days be clear about that in the contract. But when you discuss these issues inside you should also discuss what you do if the payment is late and our A/R or Credit department plans on putting the customer on hold. As this type of one invoice billing approach takes over more of your business volume, the payment cycle is more critical to your cash flow.

Your relationship with these customers will be better and stronger. It will probably be a condition where they are more dependent upon your services, including drivers as well as the service and maintenance. Planning cash flow is going to be easier, and since more cash comes in early in the contracts, you will have to be judicious in allocating the additional revenue.

Controls and Control Numbers

Just like with equipment maintenance, there must be standard control points in monitoring the contracts. One method of doing this has been discussed earlier, called control numbers. These numbers, frequently the serial number or contract number, allows you to identify all of the transactions posted to the general ledger related to one specific unit or contract. With this amount of detail you will be able to compare your actual income and expenses to the estimate that you worked out in Chapter 4. Be sure that in grouping the categories from the estimate that you have similar grouped information from the general ledger or some management reporting system.

Details That Must Be Kept

Income, cost of operations, cost of labor, vehicle expenses, depreciation, interest, mileage, and loan values for the equipment are but a few of the various items that must be tracked in some fashion for good accounting and management of a fleet of equipment units. Your best controls will be driven from the results that you know you must achieve.

Certainly you are concerned about profitability for the contract and individual units. So you want an income statement that shows income for a contract and all related expenses. Similarly you would want to analyze the same issues for each unit included in a contract. Several other areas might be of interest to you like income statements by customer (they may eventually have more than one contract), or customer location. This statement by customer location will help you analyze which locations are more profitable, have more abuse and have excess equipment. Just looking at what you need for management will help you decide what information will be necessary to create these reports. You will want to consult with your accounting people and those who oversee your computer system to make sure that these general and specific bits of information either are being tracked or can be tracked for these segmented cost centers.

Overtime Billing

In some contracts you might structure regular billing each month with overtime or excess hours billing each quarter or semi-annually. When you get ready to do this, it should be an outgrowth of your analysis meetings. Discuss the possibility that like in a rental contract extra hours may be used in the early part of the contract but balance out in the future. If you expect this condition, you might want to discuss the options with the customer. In fact, you probably would create good customer relations if you sat down with the customer at the first billing and hand delivered the invoice. At the first quarterly (or reconciliation billing for overtime), you should plan on meeting with the customer to discuss all of the causes for the extra hours.

Internal Billing

As mentioned earlier there are various accounting procedures for Fleet Management. No matter what method is being utilized, you should be aware of the effect of internal billing on sales, COGS, and gross profit volumes. Billing the customer generates an income transaction. Eventually, when you perform work on the equipment in that particular customer's fleet, you need to post the activity through your computer and accounting systems in order to reflect the usage of the parts, labor, mileage, etc. These resources have been consumed and should be reflected as such in your accounting. You probably are also tracking the productivity of technicians as a function of hours worked versus hours "billed." All of these features are generally a function of billing. But when you are doing work on equipment that the customer is paying one "fixed rate" for, then you generally handle this through "internal billing."

Internal billing has no effect on year end taxes. Standard procedures are for the accountant to eliminate these transactions from the "inter-department charges and income" before calculating taxes. But during the year they are recognized as internal income and expenses for management purposes. In this fashion the service department, who manages all of the technicians, can recognize income for the work they perform for the rental department, and rental can record income for the units they provide to the service department.

Monitoring & Dealer Reporting

There are two major reasons to monitor each Fleet Management contract. The first is to measure the profitability of the contract to the dealership and to identify areas in which improvements must be made. The second is to present to the customers an accurate account of their costs under the contract, all savings incurred, and areas in which improvements to them can be made. Therefore, in this section you'll examine internal reporting and external reporting in terms of the elements to include and how to analyze performance.

Internal Reports

The most important issue to examine is the total profitability of the contract, compared to the financial model benchmarks outlined in Chapter 4. Obviously, in some years the units will be older and require more service, and early on in the contract the administrative expenses may be high due to new processes, but overall you should achieve benchmark performance each year. Now examine the benchmark performance again with regard to a contract example.

Table 42: Fleet Management Financial Model

	Acquisition Cost		Usage Cost			Administrative Cost	
	Units	Rental	Units	Service	Parts	G&A (regular)	G&A (Fleet Mgmt)
Revenue	100%	100%	100%	100%	100%		100%
COGS	85%	55%	100%	35%	65%		0%
Gross Profit	15%	45%	0%	65%	35%		100%
Total Exp.	85% of GP	20%	-	35%	15%	10% of rental, parts, & service	100%
Net Profit	15% of GP	25%	0%	30%	20%	(10%)	0%

Applying the example from Chapter 4, Table 27, model performance is:

Table 43: Example Fleet at Benchmark Performance

	Acquisition Cost		Usage Cost			Administrative Cost	
	Units	Rental	Units	Service	Parts	G&A (regular)	G&A (Fleet Mgmt)
Revenue	295,200	N/A	1,000	140,100	36,000		23,600
COGS	262,800	N/A	1,000	49,000	23,400		0
Gross Profit	32,400	N/A	0	91,100	12,600		23,600
Total Exp.	27,500	N/A	-	49,100	5,400	17,600	23,600
Net Profit	4,900	N/A	0	42,000	7,200	(17,600)	0

Therefore, total net profit at benchmark performance is $36,500. Your internal reports should give you this information as well. That also could be expressed as $36,500 divided by the total revenue equals 7.36% of profit on sales.

Track the information that follows: acquisition, usage, and administrative costs, and warranty and non-contract items:

Table 44: Monitoring Acquisition Cost

Year	Depre-ciation	Interest	Days of Rental	Cost of Rental	Acquisition Expenses[6]	Total Acquisition Cost & Exp.

---

[6] If you have enough Fleet Management contracts to have a specialized purchaser or department, these expenses should be available. If not, estimate acquisition expense by calculating the percent of total sales (and rental expense where applicable) that the Fleet Management contract makes up, and assign that portion of the department expenses, excluding salesforce compensation.

Table 45: Monitoring Fleet Usage Cost

Date	Hours of Operator Training	Cost of Trainer	Other Fleet Usage Costs & Expenses	Total Fleet Usage Cost & Expenses

Table 46: Monitoring Service Usage Cost

Date	Unit	PM Labor Dollars	PM Labor Hours	Repair Labor Dollars	Repair Labor Hours	Travel Dollars	Travel Hours	Travel Miles	Total Service Expenses[7]	Total Service Cost & Exp.

---

[7] Benefits assigned to the labor dollars spent, service overhead personnel related to Fleet Management, and all Fleet Management service operating and occupancy expenses should be determined or estimated.

Table 47: Monitoring Parts Usage Cost

Date	Unit	Parts Retail Price	Parts Cost	Parts Expenses	Total Parts Costs & Expenses

Table 48: Monitoring Administrative Cost

Year	Total Allocated G&A Expense	Total Administration Cost for Fleet Management	Total Administrative Cost

Table 49: Monitoring Cost vs. Revenue

	Actual (from preceding tables)	Estimate (from benchmarks)	Variance
Revenue			
Acquisition Cost			
Usage Cost - Units			
Usage Cost - Service			
Usage Cost - Parts			
Administrative Cost			
Total Cost			
Profit			

Use the analysis above to determine where you are outperforming the contract and where improvements must be made.

If acquisition cost is higher than expected, refer back to your replacement cycle. Are you on track? If units are being replaced faster, why? Sort Table 47 by unit to determine which units may not need replacement yet despite the schedule.

If equipment usage cost is too high, compare the actual operator training hours with your original estimate. Are you spending too much time training, or is the cost per hour higher than expected? Or did an unforeseen event at the customer site lead to needing additional training? Perhaps you can negotiate compensation from the customer if this is the case.

If service usage cost is too high, examine the following issues first:

Warranty Recovery

From the perspective of good service and expense controls you will want to track all warranty claims. You need to know that it is covered, that it is filed, that it has been approved, and credit for the claim has been received. Warranty claims are very much like working with customers in Accounts Receivables. They pay well when they are contacted early; they go bankrupt if you are contacting them 90 days after sending the bill. With warranty claims they need to be filed in a timely manner and then followed up regularly. This chart following will help you keep track of what claims have been filed, acknowledged, and credit received.

Table 50: Tracking Warranty Claims

Warranty Claims

Date Filed	Labor Hours	Labor Dollars	Parts Billed	Claim Paid	Unpaid Claim Amount
Totals					

Abuse And Other Non-Contract Service

After handling warranties, you will want to track the amount of non-contract or abuse billing that has occurred for any contract. Customers expect no additional charges, and anything that develops extra billing is going to raise a red flag. This chart will help you begin to structure how you are going to track these extra charges and should prompt you to analyze what is causing them.

Table 51: Tracking Non-contract Items

Non-Contract

Abuse Labor Hours	Abuse Labor Dollars	Non Con-tract Dollars	Non Contract Hours
Totals			

If either warranties or non-contract labor is not being reim-bursed, the issue lies with administration. The costs should be billed and tracked and either paid or written off as uncollectible.

If those costs are being collected, examine all segments of labor cost by hour and by dollar to determine where adjustments must be made. Technician productivity should not be overlooked when analyzing service performance.

Categories	Hours		
	Actual	Estimated	Variance
OM/PM Labor			
Repair Labor			
Travel Labor			
Abuse			
Non-Contract			
Rework			
Total			

Table 52: Monitoring Service Segments by Hour

Categories	Dollar		
	Actual	Estimated	Variance
OM/PM Labor			
Repair Labor			
Travel Labor			
Abuse			
Non-Contract			
Rework			
Total			

Table 53: Monitoring Service Segments by Dollar

From these analyses, you can determine whether the PM visits should be increased or decreased or assigned to a more or less senior technician. You can also determine whether a closer look needs to be given to units high in repairs and perhaps make adjustments to your replacement cycle plans. Finally, these analyses will pinpoint issues such as travel and that your planning of PM's and repairs is important.

If parts usage is too high, again look at the service analysis. Are PM's being scheduled too often, leading to automatic replacement of some parts too early? Are PM's scheduled too infrequently, leading to part failure and unscheduled downtime?

If administrative cost is too high, examine your Fleet Management structure. Do you have personnel or other resources dedicated to Fleet Management before they're affordable? Are expenses being allocated unfairly? Remember that the administrative fee for the contract should pay for all specialized Fleet Management administrative functions, while rental, parts and service revenue pays for normal G&A expenses related to the revenue stream. There should be more than enough revenue dollars allocated to administration.

In addition to examining total profitability in each segment, you should set up your database or spreadsheet so that information can be sorted by:

- Customer
- Contract
- Model
- Serial Number
- Customer Site or Location
- Shift
- Technician

External Reports

These are the reports you will be reviewing with the customer on a regular basis. They should be clear, well documented, and relevant to the customer's savings. You should plan who will present the reports, how they will be presented, and what documentation should be left with the customer. There are several reports that should be generated and shared that need no further explanation:

- Abuse billing by location
- Fleet utilization by location vs. annual budgeted items
- On-going product problems and resolution
- General contract performance vs. plan (income, margin, cost, profit)
- Results of ongoing user satisfaction surveys
- Service response time

In addition, consider Comparison to Guaranteed Save (if applicable), Response Time Report, and Contract Equipment Downtime Report, all described here.

Comparison to "Guaranteed Save"

In many contracts there is a commitment to the amount of savings a customer may expect to see at certain time periods during the contract. If this condition exists in your contract, it has been laid out in the proposal and contract papers. You should establish how you are going to track these savings and what the method of calculation is. Frequently they begin with a base period for comparison. This might be the first quarter or year of the contract experience. It might be that your previous experience servicing the customer, or their detailed history which you have reviewed and understand is very accurate and you want to use it for your base of comparison.

A sample chart of what the commitment might be is shown below:

	Baseline Definition	Year 1	Year 2	Year 3	Year 4	Year 5	Year 6	Total Saving from Baseline
Acquisition	$	X%	X%	X%	X%	X%	X%	X%
Usage	$	X%	X%	X%	X%	X%	X%	X%
Administration	$	X%	X%	X%	X%	X%	X%	X%

Table 54: Guaranteed Save Example

This type of material should be planned into your monthly or quarterly meetings with the customer. Continuously review with them where you and they are with respect to the contract and your commitments

Comparison to Performance Standards

Your service to your customers is very good. If it wasn't, you never would have had the opportunity to even quote a Fleet Management contract, much less win the contract from the competition. But now you have commitments on the response time that you must live up to. It is very advisable that you establish a method of measuring the response time for all contracts. In many computer systems, this can be done by customer or bill-to/ship-to information on the service work orders.

Response Time			
Month or Date	Actual Average	Committed Average	Variance
Contract Average To Date			

Table 55: Response Time

Collect this information and post it for all people involved to monitor. This might include sending copies of the chart or a graph of actual and variances to the customer. Again this should be an item to consider including in your periodic meetings with the customer.

Contract Equipment Downtime			
Month or Date	**Actual Average**	**Committed Average**	**Variance**
Contract Average To Date			

Table 56: Contract Equipment Down Time

Response time is very different than measuring the actual time that a customer is out of production because a piece of equipment is not available. Certain conditions you should consider measuring are:

- when the customer called
- when the equipment actually went out of commission
- when the technician arrived on site
- when the equipment was placed back in service
- OR when a replacement unit was placed in service

Summary

The administration of the Fleet Management contract is the control of profit and the monitoring of your accuracy in estimating a good deal. From this chapter, you should have developed a method of evaluating the profitability of each contract. Some of the areas that you will have looked at are the acquisition charges, the usage cost and the administration overhead. If all of these areas are not taken care of, you are not developing a balance in your vision of the relationship. You are taking over all of the responsibilities of the fleet from the customer. You must make money to be able to afford to continue these functions. Evaluating the productivity of the fleet is just as important as measuring that of the technicians. The monitoring of a contract is an on-going process and more contracts will be added to the functions. It is imperative that you develop a consistent process that manages by exception but has access to all of the details that need to be controlled.

Conclusion

The goal of the Fleet Management Book is to act as a reference for dealers engaged in the process of pricing, selling, or implementing Fleet Management contracts. The book provides a strategic and operational look at:

- Determining the appropriate accounts to target, based on their characteristics
- Approaching those accounts using a method suitable for your dealership
- Performing customer analyses to identify current costs and appropriate fleet mix
- Developing pricing based on appropriate fleet size and mix, and financial benchmark performance
- Structuring the proposal to include all necessary elements and to act as a sales tool
- Performing the initial actions necessary to implement a Fleet Management contract
- Planning the ongoing functions necessary to perform to the contract and financial benchmark levels

The book should also inspire those dealerships not engaged in Fleet Management to embrace the profit potential available. Imagine all of your current customers contracting you to:

- Supply 100% of their equipment management (and perhaps other equipment as well)
- Perform 100% of the repair and maintenance on those units
- Provide 100% of the parts necessary to service the units
- Furnish 100% of the rental units needed
- Train 100% of their operators at a schedule that you set, and agreeing to a price that will generate:
  - o 15% gross profit on units
  - o 45% gross profit on rentals
  - o 65% gross profit on service

- o 35% gross profit on parts
- o and paying an administration fee on top of it all

Image half of your current customers in contract, or even one-third.

Imagine the profits!

Hoshin Program

DEALER PROCEDURE BOOK

Contents

Overview

The purpose of the Hoshin Program is to change the mix of dealer accounts to be weighed more heavily with high margin, high parts usage, equipment. There are multiple benefits of this program to the dealer:

- Increased total unit gross profit, leading to a higher allowance for sales expenses (based on target expenses as a percent of gross profit)

- Increased parts revenue

- Increased service revenue (dependent on capturing the increased potential)

- Increased opportunity to capture total customer potential through Fleet Management or lease with maintenance programs

The strategy by which to enact this program at the dealer level is to maintain current accounts while targeting additional accounts that fit the strategy criteria. The section in this book entitled 'Targeting Seminar Participants - Characteristics of Target Accounts' includes guidelines on identifying target accounts.

While your manufacturer works to build awareness in the target segments, relationships must be built by the dealers with their target accounts. The entry strategy proposed by the Hoshin Program calls for a one-half day seminar planned and marketed by the dealership for the targeted accounts. The seminar that should be facilitated by a third party familiar with the industry, will be aimed at increasing the knowledge of the evolution of the equipment process, the categories of equipment cost, and how the Fleet Management process affects the shareholder value. Participants will be taught the four phases of product maturity in equipment applications, and will identify their current phase.

For each phase the facilitator or manufacturer will present a description of the analysis methodology. Therefore, participants will begin to understand the way in which your methodologies could help them analyze their current needs, leading to either innovation or improvement of the existing process. The review or control step for each phase will then be discussed, along with a PMI evaluation (the Pluses, Minuses, and Interesting aspects of each phase). Copies of the subject matter are included in this book.

Finally, for each phase, the dealership will be expected to present at least one case history, in which a customer in that particular buying phase either innovated or improved its materials handling process. Details on how to develop and present the case history material are included in the section on preparing seminar materials.

This procedure book outlines the process by which to plan the seminar, including choosing the location, booking meeting space, and preparing meeting materials. A Meeting Space Comparison Form and a Checklist for Contracts are included as tools for the meeting planning, along with a general Program Checklist for general reference. In addition, promoting the seminar is addressed, in terms of the most effective way to approach potential participants and preparing the invitation package. You have also included a worksheet to estimate the cost of holding the seminar, which will be useful when budgeting for sales promotions.

The final section of this book addresses the follow through necessary to compliment the program, aimed at scheduling an on-site analysis of the target fleet. The results of that analysis, along with the target's current product phase will lead to a proposal which may include a simple purchase, maintenance plans, lease or rental plans, or complete outsourcing to the dealership in the form of Fleet Management.

Although the ultimate goal of the Hoshin program is to penetrate the target accounts, this procedure book addresses only the steps through the seminar follow-up. The individual nature of the on-site analyses and resulting proposals necessitate addressing those issues in programs specific to each scenario.

Targeting Seminar Participants

There are four steps to targeting seminar participants, outlined in this section.

Step 1: Identify target accounts.

Step 2: Group target accounts by potential seminar targets and non-seminar targets.

Step 3: Determine appropriate mix of seminar participants.

Step 4: Identify target seminar participants.

Characteristics Of Target Accounts

Target accounts use equipment representing high margin and frequent parts replacement and have a high growth potential.

This section discussed how to determine *your* target accounts.

Probably your manufacturer has completed a research study to profile key industry segments that fit the goals of the Hoshin Program as described in the Overview. The result of that study could be the identification of four target segments:

- Food Products
- Industrial/Electric
- Metals
- Warehouse/Storage
- Landscapers
- Arborists

- Apartment/Condo Complexes
- Golf Courses
- Etc.
-

The first step in targeting accounts is to examine the current and potential client database for your territory and identify those in these industries. If your database is not extensive enough for this step, request the information of your manufacturer. They'll have a list of companies by these SIC codes for your territory. The next step is to determine what other accounts might be targeted. The criteria to use in evaluating your database is as follows:

- Users of certain categories of equipment (each industry will be different)

- A and B size fleets that purchase a minimum of 30 units annually
- Fleets that are less than 20% your brand
- Accounts that have a significant growth potential

All current and potential accounts that fit the industry criteria or at least three of the four other criteria should be included in the target customer group. This group can vary greatly in size between dealerships, so no parameters are set. All should be approached either to attend the seminar as a group, or on an individual basis. See the next section, grouping target accounts, for instruction on which accounts to invite to the seminar, and who to approach in a different way.

Grouping Target Accounts

Some target accounts should be approached to attend the Hoshin seminar. Others may more appropriately be approached individually.

This section discusses *which accounts will benefit the most* from attending the seminar and which accounts will *benefit the dealership* by attending.

The real issue to consider is whether some target accounts will be disruptive or potentially subversive in a seminar setting. That might happen if they already have strong feelings for or against your dealership, your brand, or the services to be presented. Here you examine each situation individually.

1. **Your Dealership** - If the contacts at a target account already have a very positive opinion about your dealership, they should certainly be invited to the seminar. In fact, accounts that fit into this category should be approached for seminar material. Create a success story around their experience with your dealership and ask them if they will contribute a quote, or if they will say a few words at the seminar to verify your story.

On the other hand, if a target account has had a negative experience with your dealership and still holds a negative opinion of your services, be careful about including them in this forum. One negative comment either during the seminar or in the hallway during the break could lose you a potential account. In this situation, judge the personality of the contact as well as the experience. Was the negative experience quite a while ago and the issues well resolved? Is the contact open-minded, and will listen despite past experience?

2.   Manufacturer - Contacts with strong positive feelings about the manufacturer are also very valuable at the seminar. Those that are more negative about your brand should not be dismissed automatically though. To most accounts, timely and accurate service support is as important or more important than the manufacturer when making acquisition decisions. Therefore, their feelings about your manufacturer are less important than their feelings about your dealership.

In addition, the issues to be discussed in the seminar, such as tracking costs, ROI, evolution of the market, and Fleet Management are educational for every account. Realizing that your dealership and your manufacturer understand these issues and can help them in maximizing their ROI could go a long way to improve their opinion of your brand.

3.   **Services** - Some of your target accounts will have preconceived opinions about outsourcing their Fleet Management or contracting for lease with maintenance. In fact, all will have some preference in terms of how they do business with their equipment supplier(s). This seminar is geared, however, toward accounts in all buying phases, from a simple purchase of units and parts (performing their own service), to complete outsourcing. Regardless of their preferences, each account should benefit from the information provided and should leave understanding the benefit your dealership can provide them.

Determining the Appropriate Mix

Participants will not be receptive to a learning experience in the presence of their competitors.

This section reviews the appropriate mix of accounts.

You've grouped your target account list into a potential seminar group and a group that should be approached individually. Now it's time to examine the mix of participants. The most important issue is to *avoid having competitors attend*.

Because specific industries are being targeted, there will probably be competitors on your target seminar list. At this point they should be identified. However, don't automatically assume that companies in the same industry are competitors. Depending on the size of your territory, the companies' locations, their actual product lines, and their actual markets, there may be very few competitors on your list. If you aren't sure, use the following guidelines:

1. **Ask Your Contact** - If the account is a current customer, or if someone in your dealership has a relationship with the contact that makes it possible, asking is the most obvious step. Explain that you plan to hold an informational seminar for area businesses, but you wish to avoid inviting competing firms. Not only will you get your information, but the contact will appreciate your sensitivity to the issue and may feel obliged to attend.

2. **Research the Company** - If the account is new to you and you're unable or uncomfortable asking, obtain all the public

information available about the company. Promotional information such as brochures, advertisements in the newspaper, trade journal, or yellow pages, and other distributed material will give you insight into their specific products and services, and their market. For instance, you'll be able to differentiate between the specialty business and the general line business, the local producer and the nationwide supplier. By comparing the information of several companies, you'll have a good idea as to competitors or possible competitors. In addition, the information you gather will give you insight into how you can best serve the account.

Once you've determined competitors in your group, list them in descending order in terms of participant target. Preference should be given to the company with the most potential to you, whether that be because of their low current share, total fleet size, or positive attitude toward your dealership. Keep in mind that if your top choice to attend chooses not to, there may be time to invite another. In addition, if attendance is high at your first seminar, there is no reason not to hold a second in order to include the majority of targets.

Identifying Target Participants

Strategic decision makers are the target audience of this seminar.

This section discusses how to identify your invitees.

Now that you have a list of accounts to invite, determine *how many* people from each company to invite, and *who* is appropriate. In general, invite more than one person from each company. In most cases, several people are involved in deciding how to structure equipment acquisitions (buying, renting, leasing, outsourcing) and the timing of such acquisitions. In those cases having more than one person involved in the seminar is obviously beneficial.

Inviting the appropriate people is a vital aspect of the planning process. The audience of this seminar should be the people to whom the strategic nature of this seminar is most important. That may include the **VP of Distribution** or Warehousing, the **VP of Operations**, the **General Manager**, and the **principal**. Try to invite a financial contact as well as the usual operations contact. Invite any that apply, and ask your normal contact for other suggestions. In addition, the normal contact should be invited. Make sure to always address the invitations to the actual people you want to attend and never to just the position title or to the company in general.

At this point you should have three lists:

- Names and addresses of invitees to the Hoshin seminar

- Names of alternate companies (competitors of the invitees) that may be invited if the invitees decline, may be invited to a second seminar, or may be approached individually
- Names of target accounts that will be approached individually

Before inviting participants, you now need to decide on a time and place for the seminar, and prepare an invitation. The next section 'Meeting Planning' will lead you through that process.

Meeting Planning

There are four steps to meeting planning, as follows. If your office is accustomed to holding meetings for multiple clients, this information will seem fundamental. It is to be used as a guideline with those new to off-site meeting planning for multiple participants.

Step 1: Choose a meeting location.

Step 2: Book meeting space.

Step 3: Determine and contract for catering needs.

Step 4: Prepare meeting materials for participants.

Choose a Meeting Location

The easier it is to reach the seminar site, the more likely the invitee will attend..

This section lists the things to consider when choosing a location.

The logistics of the meeting must be planned now in order to create the invitation package and begin marketing. The first step is choosing a location: state, city, and conference center or hotel.

You all know that convenience is key these days. Although you are offering the invitee a service in terms of information, you'll still have to sell the seminar. That said, invitees are much more likely to attend a session that is a short distance away than one held several hours away. In particular, if you plan a morning seminar, the commute must be practical to make in the morning.

1. **Examine your territory**. Are the accounts very far away from each other, or are they grouped around a specific city? Are there two distinct groupings of these accounts? If you have any simple mapping software, import your target account database and geocode by zip code or city. The seminar location may then become obvious, or it may become clear that two seminars would best serve the accounts due to geography.

2.   Analyze the road system. How easy is it for each of the target accounts to reach a central location? If possible, choose a location that is within two hours of every invitee. Certainly, if the meeting is held in the morning, people will not drive longer than that to attend a ½ day seminar. In the afternoon, they might be willing to travel three hours, but not necessarily.

3.   Choose a city. Based on the geography and account locations, the city location should be an easy choice. Keep in mind that a city will have more choice as to meeting space than a more rural area. Flexibility in terms of group size and availability of space will be critical to the planning. Those accounts that opt not to attend, whether based on convenience of location, seminar date, or lack of interest, can be approached individually at a later time.

4.   Investigate meeting space. Once a city has been chosen, hotels and conference centers must be investigated to determine that there is *affordable*, *appropriate* space *available* for the date you need. First, choose a date and time, then book meeting space.

Booking Meeting Space

There are five steps to obtaining the most appropriate and affordable facility for this program.

Set the Date and Time

Estimate the Number of Attendees

Review the A/V and Catering Needs

Call Facilities and Compare

Fax Requirements to the Chosen Site.

1. Date & Time - Before you can reserve meeting space or even determine the cost of the space, you must set a date and time. Coordinate with your manufacturer's representative who will be attending, the outside facilitator, and your own personnel. In general, holiday weeks and Friday afternoons are not successful in terms of attendance. In addition, during the first days of each month financial and operational reporting is due, making that a difficult time for many to leave the office.

2. Number of Attendees - Before calling hotels or conference centers, you'll want to estimate the number of attendees you expect and write down your requirements on the 'Meeting Space Comparison Form' provided. First, write down the name of the event, the city, and the date and time on the form.

To estimate the number of attendees, determine how many companies you are inviting and what percentage of them are current customers. Determine the *low end of the attendee range* by assuming that only one-fourth of the current customer accounts will send one person. That is, if you have 100 accounts listed, and 60 of those are current customers, 15 attendees is the lowest expected affirmative response. Add to that the facilitator, the manufacturer's representative, and the expected attendees from your company. The total is the low end of the attendee range.

To estimate the *high end of the* attendee range, assume that 50% of all invited accounts are able and willing to send two representatives. Therefore, of the 100 accounts invited, 50 of them send on average 2 people. Adding the same number of additional attendees as in the above example gives the high end of the expected attendee range.

Unfortunately, the range calculated here might still be too large to successfully book meeting room space. Using the example above and adding approximately 10 non-account attendees, the range becomes 25 - 110 people. A room large enough to hold 100 will seem empty with only 25, and a room that is comfortable for 50 will be much too crowded for 110. Therefore, the flexibility of the hotel or conference center, and the number of attendees from your own dealership will be key. For now, fill in the number of invitees, the approximate attendee range, and the midpoint of the attendee range as the expected number of attendees, on the Meeting Comparison Form. (In our example, the midpoint would be $(110-25) \div 2 = 42$.)

3. Audio-visual & Catering Needs - When you compare the cost of various facilities, you may find room costs to be similar, but one facility may charge for AV equipment while the others do not. In addition, some facilities might waive or reduce the meeting room fee if catering charges exceed a certain amount. Therefore, know your needs before you begin calling.

Catering needs must be determined based on the seminar timing. A morning seminar usually begins with a continental breakfast and may or may not include lunch. An afternoon seminar does not usually include lunch but may involve a reception after the event. Although you'll want to keep costs reasonable, this opportunity for socializing with the contacts should be maximized, and contact immediately following the seminar will allow you to get some instant feedback. Regardless of other catering decisions, a morning or afternoon break is mandatory. It does not have to involve food, but beverages must be provided and coffee freshened.

In terms of audiovisual equipment, an overhead projector and screen will be necessary as well as a flip chart and markers. If the presentation by your dealership requires other equipment, list that on the form as well. In order to compare facilities and book meeting space, no final AV or catering decisions must be made at this point. Knowing basic needs, however, will help you determine the most affordable and appropriate facility.

4. Compare Facilities - Begin your search with a well known, better than average chain, such as a Marriott, Hyatt, Renaissance, Four Seasons, or Sheraton. This will give you a standard to go by for the area and your needs. Then choose at least two others either from that list or of a more local variety. If they don't have space available for your needs, ask the contact to refer another facility. If they do have space available, the questions below can be a guideline to get the comparison information you need. Make sure to note all price and flexibility information on the comparison form.

- What is the price of your meeting room for this group size?
- How many will it hold in a **classroom style** setup?
- If the actual group size changes dramatically, how flexible is your facility in order to accommodate the change?
- Do you charge for the use of the audiovisual equipment needed?
- Do you reduce/waive the meeting room fee if catering charges reach a certain level?
- What is your cancellation policy?
- What is your billing policy? Do you require a deposit? Is total payment due at the time of the event? Do you bill after the event?

If the terms sound reasonable, ask if you can *hold the room*, while you continue your research. Most facilities will provide a hold for up to a week, depending on the season and vacancy rate. Call a minimum of three facilities to assure a good representation. Then rate your options based on the information you've gathered. ***Before requesting a contract for any facility, visit the site.*** Most meeting space coordinators will give you a tour themselves, to acquaint you with their facility. Whenever possible, take advantage of this opportunity unless you're already familiar with the location. Brochure pictures can be deceiving, and this seminar will be a reflection of your dealership.

5. Fax Requirements - When you've decided on a facility, fax your contact a request for a contract. In your fax, repeat the date, time, number of attendees (approximate), AV requirements, price quoted, and group name as you would like it to appear on their listings. In addition, include:

- **A description of the meeting setup you require**. When using a classroom setup, facilities will normally use either 8 or 6-foot tables. You've all attended meetings that were uncomfortable due to the close quarters of the setup. If using 8-foot tables, 3 attendees to a table is appropriate. No more than 2 people should be assigned to a 6-foot table.
- **Other facility requirements**. Normally the facility will supply pens, paper, water, and hard candy to each table, upon request.
- **A request for banquet menus.** In order to arrange catering services you need to see the possible menus.
- **Any special services, waivers, or price reductions that you negotiated.**

When you receive the contract, review it against the 'Checklist for Contracts' supplied here. Note all cancellation dates and fees. If the arrangements are correct and the terms appropriate, sign the contract immediately and send it back to them, so that the room is not lost.

Catering Needs

Food relaxes people and fosters the feeling that this is a social event.

This section discusses how to fulfill your catering needs in terms of *timing* your communications, *choosing a menu*, and signing the *Banquet Event Order*.

Timing - Once the contract has been signed, you can begin communication with the catering department. While the meeting room should be booked as soon as a date for the seminar has been set, meals and breaks need to be set up only one month (or less) prior to the meeting. However, because there can be delays in receiving menus, banquet event orders, and the like, starting early is usually beneficial.

Choosing a Menu - At this point, you already should have a good idea of your needs in terms of meals and breaks. Ask your catering contact for their appropriate meal, break, and reception menus. They will describe the offerings and prices per person. If you don't see a simple menu offered, such as a deli buffet lunch or an hors d'oeuvre reception, ask your contact. Quite often you can create your own menu to fit your needs. In addition, try to negotiate for break beverages to be billed on a 'per consumption' basis, rather than a flat fee per person. Normally the per person rate far exceeds what people actually consume, especially when water is provided on the tables.

When you've made your selections, fax them in to the catering department. Make sure that they are aware of your room setup, AV needs, and other facility requirements, as all of that information should be included in the Banquet Event Order that they send you.

Banquet Event Order - When you receive the Banquet Event Order, review it against the Contract Checklist provided. Note the last date to make changes to the attendee number, and heed it carefully. You'll pay for the number of attendees listed on the finalized BEO on the date they set. On that date, always estimate 5% fewer attendees in terms of food requirements than your actual count. However, make sure they set the room for as many attendees as your actual count.

Sample Menu (Special Notes and Comments)

Breakfast

Assorted Cereals: Total Raisin Bran, Special K, Corn Flakes, Granola and Yogurt

Assorted Fruit: Apples, Bananas, Raisins, Strawberries, and Seasonal Berries

Assorted Bagels: Blueberry, Cinnamon, and Plain

Assorted Muffins: Banana, Cranberry, and Bran

Whole Boiled Shell Eggs

Coffee and Assorted Hot Tea

Lunch

Caesar Salad or Chef Salad

Assorted Sandwich Stacks*

Assorted Breads

Pickle Spears

Chips, Pasta, Potato Salad or Cole Slaw

Iced Tea, Water, and Coffee

Break

Popcorn, Mixed Nuts, M&M's

* See note about Sandwich Stacks on the next page

Helpful Hints:

- Be sure the breakfast you offer is not exclusively starch. Pastries are high in sugar, which will give your audience a quick energy boost followed by a sugar crash that may make it difficult to maintain concentration.
- Whole boiled shelled eggs are a great way to add protein to breakfast. Shell eggs, high in protein, slow the effects of carbohydrate highs and lows.
- Ask your caterer to supply items that are made from whole grains. The idea is to allow for the meal to be digested in a manner that is conducive to learning.
- You don't always have to use the catering department of the facility that is hosting your event. Check the prices of local caterers.
- **Bonus hint**: Check the price of having a personal chef cater your event. If the facility you are using has a banquet hall and kitchen but does not provide catering, on-site catering with a personal chef is a great way to go. The facility will cost less, as will the catering. Think outside the box, but get references.
- Invite the participants to join you for breakfast a half hour before the beginning of the conference. This is a time to put the audience at ease in an informal setting. It is also a time for information gathering by the presenter.
- Unless you know your audiences' taste, stick with classic salads. While tossed garden salads are the safest way to go, Caesar or Chef Salads give a greater perception of professionalism.
- Sandwich Stacks* are a great way to give the audience choice with little or no additional cost. Have your caterer plate assorted meats – Ham, Roast Beef, and Turkey— with cheeses and lettuce, tomato, and onion in stacks.

Have the assorted breads on the side. Your guests can then build the sandwich that he or she prefers. Not only do your guests get what they want on the sandwich, but also he or she gains a sense of empowerment. It is a great way to add an addition layer of participation to your event.

Cornell Colbert, Sodexho International at Memorial Health System, Director of Nutrition Service, Memorial Hospital North, Colorado Springs, CO

Meeting Materials

The professional quality of the seminar materials gives participants a definite impression of the dealership.

This section discusses the needs of the dealership to produce the necessary materials.

As the seminar draws near, you'll be preparing name badges, tent cards, and seminar content material for attendees. If your dealership is not accustomed to creating these materials, make sure you have the capability in-house, or investigate printing services.

To create name badges and tent cards in-house, make sure you have a good quality printer and word processing or other software capable of the task. You may wish to have all seminar material printed on special paper with your logo or other design specific to this program. If so, have the name badges and tent cards match the design. Starts early as you receive replies and always have extra blank materials at the seminar for unexpected guests.

Content meeting materials are discussed in the section entitled 'Preparing Meeting Materials'. At this point, the invitees have been selected, and the logistics have been determined. The next section addresses how to market the seminar for the best turnout.

Promoting the Seminar

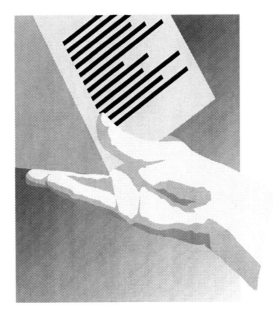

Promoting the seminar is the most important step in making the program successful. The process you recommend to promote the program is as follows:

Step 1: Prepare and send a seminar brochure to all invitees.

Step 2: Present program to salespeople and dealership.

Step 3: Contact target participants personally or by telephone to judge and increase interest.

Step 4: Send invitations to interested targets.

Step 5: Follow-up with interested targets.

The Seminar Brochure

The three elements that must be included in the brochure are:

- Why the invitees were targeted
- What they will gain from attending
- What you expect from them.

Here you examine each of these issues and how to present them.

The brochure is the initial contact with the target and serves to create interest in the program. It should make it clear to the addressee that the seminar is primarily an educational effort, not a sales effort, and that it is primarily strategic in nature, not operational. However, the targets should understand that they will develop action items that will enable them to improve their business process immediately, and that the information is not strictly theoretical.

Why did they invite me? The brochure or a cover letter should answer this question immediately. If the invitation package is not personalized in any way, the invitee will treat it as any other piece of direct mail and may not even read it. Use the behavioral objectives, the strategic intent, and the shareholder value chain found in the seminar material to help you frame your approach.

The brochure may begin as a 'Note to Preferred X Dealership Customers', stating that they have been identified as the companies most likely to understand the strategic role of Process Improvement in the Shareholder Value Chain. Or a cover letter accompanying the brochure may point out that since their company is already involved in a process improvement program in relation to other aspects of their business, that this program might be of particular interest. Another approach could be that because a target is such a valued customer, the dealership would not think of excluding them from this educational opportunity.

What will I get from it? The brochure should explain exactly what participants will gain from the seminar. The behavioral objectives and strategic intent should be included (either verbatim or paraphrased). In addition, any information that you think will be especially interesting to *your targets* should be included. The points may be taken from the details of the seminar or from your case histories. Be sure, however, not to give away information in the brochure that will make it unnecessary for the target to attend.

What do they expect from me? In the brochure, clearly state the cost of the seminar, the date and time, and the location. It is our recommendation that a cost of $150 should be assigned to the seminar, to give it credibility as an educational effort. However, during the follow-up with invitees, salespeople should give free passes or offer to waive the fee, in order to maximize participation. To avoid confusion and ill will, either all participants should pay or they should all not pay. Again, in order to maximize attendance, all fees should be waived. This issue is discussed again in the section on presenting the program to the dealership. Include in the brochure all information about refreshments provided. State that participation will be limited to ensure the most effective learning environment.

In the brochure, be sure to include a sign-up form and who to call if the invitee has questions. Send the brochures out approximately six weeks before the seminar date to ensure appropriate time for follow-up and revision of meeting space counts.

Present Program to
Salespeople & Dealership Employees

The sales force must follow-up with brochure recipients, and all dealership personnel must be aware of the seminar in order to answer questions.

How much information? Before addressing the company, determine who will be following up with each invitee, who will be responsible for collecting responses, and who you want to respond to inquiries. If the sales department will be handling all of these issues, *the rest of the company need only be informed that the seminar will take place and to whom to refer inquiries*. The simplest method of communication in this case would be to distribute a copy of the brochure to employees, along with a memo explaining inquiry and response procedure.

The sales force and any other employees who will be following up with invitees, responding to inquiries, or collecting response forms should have more education on the purpose of the seminar, its content, and the expected outcome. They should understand whom the program was designed for and how the target participants were chosen. As the dealer principal, you should present to your team the sections of this workbook that apply, and preferably have them see the seminar presented.

The key is to have all salespeople understand how *they* will benefit from a large turnout, so that they take the time to follow up with every invitee. You may offer incentives to the salespeople who obtain the largest response, or you may require the follow up in order for them to not lose existing incentives. You'll have to judge your sales force to determine whether or not they can see the long-term benefits of the program without special incentives and will work to get maximum participation.

One issue that must be clarified is the waiving of fees. The dealership could print "Complimentary Seminar Admission" passes, good for up to four people from each company. Distribute them, explaining that you don't want the target to miss the opportunity presented.

Timing - Training can be done any time between receiving the program procedure book and the receipt of the brochures by the invitees. *Make sure the employees are educated by the time brochures are mailed in order to field questions immediately.* In addition to improving the salespersons' knowledge of the program, your sales force will have informed input on success stories you may present and techniques to obtain a good participation rate.

Contact Target Participants

Increase interest and participation by approaching each
brochure recipient personally.

This section reviews the timing and
importance of the personal follow-up.

Who should contact?   Much of the contacting can be done by
the sales force, but the dealer principal and other key management personnel might approach targets of particular significance.   You must project the image that this seminar is not
simply a sales pitch and is aimed at what might be a different
level of personnel than the regular contact.   Preferably, all brochure recipients should be contacted personally.   However, if
there are time or access constraints, some can be phoned.

How?   The contact may be couched in the context of checking
to make sure they received the brochure, giving out complimentary passes, and being available to answer questions.   During
the contact, reiterate the benefits of the seminar and why you
believe they will benefit from it.   Finally, *judge their interest
level and determine whether they should be sent an official
invitation*.   The intention is that the invitations are somewhat
more exclusive than the brochure and should be sent only to
strong prospects for participation.

Timing - The contact should take place during the fourth and
fifth weeks before the event, one to two weeks after the brochure was mailed.   Those targets that seem interested should
immediately be sent an invitation.

Invitations

All invitation materials should look professional, yet person-alized.

This section discusses the elements to include in your invitations.

The Design - As soon as the brochures are designed, the invitations can be designed and printed. They should be quality invitations (such as those for a wedding), set on one side of high quality, small sized paper. The wording should be formal, such as in the sample invitation enclosed. Don't print up too many at a time, as the number of interested targets cannot be foretold. Envelopes should be hand written and stamped (don't use your postage machine!), to extend the image of exclusivity and personalization.

Include with the invitation a response card which confirms the invitee's participation. The card should request: Name of respondent, company represented, number to attend, and names of attendees. It should also restate the date, time, location, and seminar fee of $150. Respondents then can mail the card back with their complimentary pass. Be sure that the response date is included and that it gives you enough time to adjust your attendee count with the meeting facility without bringing on extra charges.

The Process - When a response is received from the brochure, note the respondent and send out an invitation. In addition, as targets are contacted, those that seem interested in the seminar should also be noted and mailed an invitation.

At this point, note the companies that are not being sent invitations, and compare it with your initial list of Alternate Invitees from the Targeting section. If a target account was put on the alternate list because a competitor was invited, and that competitor is not interested, you can now target the alternate.

Immediately send a brochure and follow-up personally a week later. If the alternate is interested, hand them an invitation and try to obtain a response immediately. The brochures should be sent to alternates during the fourth week before the seminar, and the follow-up done during the third week before. That schedule will put the alternates in line with the rest of the invitees for the final follow-up.

Final Follow-Up

The final follow-up is a last attempt to obtain participation, and thus should be done by the dealer principal, sales manager, or other management level employee.

Timing - All recipients of the brochure should have been contacted by four weeks before the seminar. All invitations should have been sent out immediately and received by three weeks before the meeting. The final follow-up should be done two weeks before the meeting with all invitation recipients who have not responded.

Purpose - The invitee may be interested in attending but is either unable due to scheduling or is unwilling due to specific reservations about the program. In these cases, the invitee may be persuaded to come or to send a replacement or may be a potential attendee at a second seminar. On the other hand, the invitee may not be interested in the program, in which case you should try to find out why.

Result - At the end of this follow-up stage, you should have a list of attendees, a list of those interested but unable to attend, and a list of those that are not interested. The length of your second list, along with any alternate invitees (from the Targeting section) that could not be invited will help you determine whether a second seminar is necessary.

Preparing Seminar Materials

The dealership must take part in the Hoshin presentation and must provide seminar materials to all attendees. The two parts of this section are:

Step 1: Seminar responsibilities of the dealership.

Step 2: Participant materials.

Dealership Seminar
Responsibilities

You must add a case for each buying phase to the seminar presentation.

This section describes the appropriate material to use.

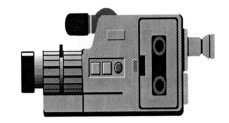

Choosing Subject Material - Your manufacturer may supply the dealership with videotape for the seminar as a tool to educate the dealership personnel. To determine the appropriate cases to use for each section, first understand the phases.

Phase I: The account is concerned with innovation in its equipment handling process, through an innovation in the ***product***. That innovation comes about because of either a change in the account or a change in the industry. The account might suddenly be large enough to *use* your equipment for the first time or to use a certain *type* to do the job in a new way. On the other hand, a new *model* might have come out, offering a new process option to the account. An alternative might include an account that simply wasn't *aware* of a process option until your dealership described it.

Taking any of those scenarios, explain the circumstances of the account, how your dealership helped the account determine their needs, the conclusion reached, and how the implemented conclusion changed the equipment process of that account.

Phase II: The account is concerned with improving the existing process still by way of the ***product*** only, through reducing product price. There should be no problem determining appropriate cases for this phase. The best example, however, will be a case in which the price point itself was deceiving to the customer when comparing several lines.

Walk through the analysis that you may have done with or for the customer such as comparing product features, warranty terms, service capability, and financing terms, as well as price. Show how a thorough analysis supplied the customer with the information needed to make the best financial choice, based on the product.

Phase III: The account is still concerned with improving the existing process through the ***product***, but is now examining the entire cost of ownership of the product. The analysis will have involved the cost of maintaining the equipment, and its estimated useful life. The process may have been to determine the appropriate time to replace a unit, or to design a rental or lease with maintenance program to minimize total cost for the account. Again, walk through your process with the account, the choice made, and how it benefited the customer.

Phase IV: At this point, the account is concerned with innovation of the process, and is willing to change their entire ***process*** to minimize the cost of equipment management as a whole. This phase would refer to a customer completely outsourcing their equipment management to a supplier. It may be that you have no experience providing this service. In that case, be honest with the participants and say that. However, you can also explain how you might work with an account that way, similar to the relationship that your manufacturer has with some large local account.

Preparing Your Presentation - Once you have determined the cases to use, prepare your presentation. There are several options to choose from, including videotaping the cases, preparing slide or overhead presentations, or preparing your text and having no visual display but what you write on flipcharts. In terms of length, you expect the details of each phase to take approximately ½ hour. Therefore, case histories can run from five to ten minutes for each phase. You may describe one case in detail or two or three more briefly.

Video: One benefit of videotaping is that your presentation is completed before the seminar, so if you are uncomfortable with or inexperienced at presentation, this may be your best option. In addition, a case that can be shown in this way gives authenticity to your story, especially if you can include testimony from the customer. Don't feel as though the tape must be of professional quality - the noise and chaos at the account site is familiar to all participants.

Slides or Overheads: If you decide to prepare overheads, try to keep them consistent in appearance to the rest of the seminar. The only exception to that is if you decide to show particular reports or surveys that you used to analyze the fleets and make recommendations. (In fact, these tools that you use would tie in very well with the rest of the presentation, and show the participants specific ways in which you could help them with their process.)

If you are using word processing software instead, make sure the font is as large enough and try to keep colors consistent. When designing overheads, remember that they shouldn't contain every word you intend to say but should highlight the points you don't want participants to miss.

Verbal: Finally, if you don't intend to prepare visual aids, prepare your case histories well. Don't allow the audience to think that you didn't put any preparation time into your material. If possible, use the flipchart to summarize important information such as cost-savings or information analyzed.

Participant Materials

Every participant in the seminar should be given a packet of information.

This section lists the items that should be included.

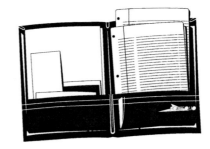

A Name Badge and Tent Card – These items were already discussed in the Meeting Planning section.

An Agenda - Type up the agenda with the meeting location and time information. Include refreshment and break information. A break should be taken after Phase I or Phase II, and should last 15 minutes. The time allocation you expect for each section is as follows:

1. Introductions - 5 min.
2. Behavioral Objectives & Strategic Intent - 10 min.
3. Shareholder Value Chain & Impact of M/H Process- 30 min.
4. Evolution of Equipment Management Process: Overview - 15 min.

       Phase I - 30 min.

       Phase II - 30 min.

       Phase III - 30 min.

       Phase IV - 30 min.

5. Participation Review - 10 min.
6. Questions & Answers - 20 min.
7. Evaluation & Close - 15 min.

Action Sheets - These are provided in this book and need only be copied. Be sure to have extra copies on hand the day of the seminar.

Evaluation Form - These are also provided and will be completed by every participant before leaving the seminar.

Seminar Follow-Up

There are two categories of follow-up that are addressed in this section.

Step 1: All seminar participants must be contacted immediately following the seminar to be thanked for their attendance and to be urged into requesting services.

Step 2: A process of follow-through must be developed for inquiries that come in due to seminar attendance.

Attendee Follow-up

Within a week of the seminar, you must mail a letter to all participants thanking them for all their attendance. Personal follow-up can then begin to market site analyses.

Thank-you Letter - Obviously, each letter must be addressed to the participant directly, and a separate letter should be sent to each participant, even if several attend from a single company. The dealer principal should write that letter.

The letter should reference the evaluation form, and state that the territory manager or other specific person will be contacting them soon if the dealership can be of help to the company (using information stated on the evaluation form). The letter may also sum up some of the positive comments received about the seminar, again via the evaluation form. Finally, the letter should make it clear that you are available to answer any questions about the seminar or about how your dealership can help participants fulfill their action plan.

Personal Follow-up - Shortly after the letters are sent, salespeople or the sales manager can begin their personal follow-up. If there weren't many participants, the sales manager may want to perform the follow-up him/herself, or work with the salesperson. If there was a very large turnout, the salespeople will need to work alone. In either case, the dealership representative should examine the evaluation form for keys to making the visit most successful. That evaluation form includes the participant's current and future buying process as well as how the dealership could help the participant attain their process improvement goals.

The purpose of the follow-up visit is not to sell a product or service but to get agreement to do an on-site analysis of the fleet. That analysis, along with the participants' stated current and future buying phase, will lead you to the appropriate proposal format.

All personal follow-up visits should take place within three weeks of the seminar.

Inquiry Follow-Up

Before the seminar takes place, a process should be developed for responding to inquiries.

With luck, the Hoshin seminar will produce more leads than any other program you've enacted. All inquiries for information, or for specific products or services could go through one person at your dealership (such as the sales manager or an administrative person), or they all may be referred to the salespeople directly.

In either case, make sure the person fielding inquiries has full knowledge of the seminar material. In addition, that person must be entirely familiar with your standard process for completing on-site fleet analyses. If no such standard process currently exists, spend time before the seminar synthesizing the processes you currently use, collecting any tools from your manufacturer that apply, and developing the process you will use in the future.

Meeting Space Comparison Form

Event:

_____

# of Invitees:

_____

Date & Time:

_____

Attendee Range:

_____

Location:

_____

Expected # of Attendees:

_____

AUDIO VISUAL NEEDS:

- ☐ OVERHEAD PROJECTOR & SCREEN
- ☐ FLIPCHART AND MARKERS
- ☐ OTHER _____

CATERING NEEDS:

- ☐ CONTINENTAL BREAKFAST
- ☐ MORNING BREAK
- ☐ LUNCH
- ☐ AFTERNOON BREAK
- ☐ RECEPTION

HOTEL/ CONFERENCE CENTER NAME:

CONTACT NAME:

PHONE:

- ☐ Meeting Room Price:
- ☐ Meeting Room Flexibility:
- ☐ Charge For Av:
- ☐ Discount On Meeting Room For Catering:
- ☐ On Hold:
- ☐ Comments:
- ☐ Hotel/ Conference Center Name:
- ☐ Contact Name:
- ☐ Meeting Room Price:
- ☐ Meeting Room Flexibility:
- ☐ Charge For Av:
- ☐ Discount On Meeting Room For Catering:

On Hold: ☐

Comments:

Checklist - Hoshin Program

TARGETING SEMINAR PARTICIPANTS:

☐ Identified target accounts (16 weeks prior)

☐ Grouped accounts by seminar and non-seminar targets (15 weeks prior)

☐ Determined appropriate seminar mix (15 weeks prior)

☐ Identified target seminar participants (15 weeks prior)

☐ Prepared list of names and addresses of invitees to the Seminar (14 weeks prior)

☐ Prepared list of alternate companies for invitation (14 weeks prior)

☐ Prepared list of target accounts to be approached individually (14 weeks prior)

MEETING PLANNING:

☐ Location chosen (13 weeks prior)

☐ Date & time coordinated and booked with all parties (12 weeks prior)

☐ Meeting space booked (12 weeks prior)

☐ Refreshments chosen (4 weeks prior)

☐ Banquet event orders signed (3 weeks prior)

☐ Name badges and tent cards prepared (1 week prior)

PROMOTING:

- ☐ Brochure developed printed & mailed (6 weeks prior)
- ☐ Marketing responsibilities determined (6 weeks prior)
- ☐ Program explained to Dealership (6 weeks prior)
- ☐ All target participants approached (4 weeks prior)
- ☐ Invitations sent & alternate invitees analyzed (4 weeks prior)
- ☐ Alternate invitees sent brochure (4 weeks prior)
- ☐ Alternate invitees approached (3 weeks prior)
- ☐ Final follow-up done (2 weeks prior)
- ☐ Responses are tallied and final counts given to meeting facility (1 week prior)
- ☐ Determination made on necessity of second seminar (2 weeks after)

SEMINAR MATERIAL PREPARED:

- ☐ Case histories chosen (5 weeks prior)
- ☐ Case material prepared (4 weeks prior)
- ☐ Agenda prepared (3 weeks prior)
- ☐ All handout material copied and packets finalized (1 week prior)

SEMINAR FOLLOW-UP:

- ☐ Thank-you letter written (1 week after)
- ☐ Thank-you letter mailed to all participants (1 week after)
- ☐ Personal follow-up visits completed (3 weeks after)
- ☐ Inquiry process developed & relayed to all dealership personnel (seminar date)

Checklist For Contracts

HOTEL/ CONFERENCE CENTER
NAME: _____

ADDRESS: _____

CONTACT NAME: _____

PHONE: _____

MEETING:

- ☐ Dates correct
- ☐ Contract signed
- ☐ Audio/visual needs included: overhead, screen, flipchart with markers
- ☐ Room setup noted
- ☐ Hard candies, water, pencils & paper included
- ☐ Number of attendees correct

LAST DAY TO CANCEL WITHOUT CHARGE IS _____

CANCELLATION FEES AFTER THAT DATE ARE _____

CATERING:

- ☐ Banquet Event Orders Signed
- ☐ Menus Correct
- ☐ Number of Attendees Correct
- ☐ Agreed on Billing practice Noted

LAST DAY TO MAKE CHANGES TO ATTENDEE COUNT IS _____

Sample Invitation

This Dealership
cordially invites you to
a special presentation of

Fleet Management Process Improvement
a Qualitative and Quantitative Approach

Presented by:
Currie Management Consultants
Sponsored by:
This Dealership
In Conjunction With:
Your Manufacturer

To be held on
Wednesday, January 21,
from one o'clock to five o'clock p.m.
Boston Hilton
50 Commonwealth Avenue
Boston, MA

The pleasure of your response is requested
by January 7.
Enrollment fee: $150 per person

Seminar Cost Worksheet

Meeting Room $_____

Audio-Visual $_____

Meeting Meals $_____

Meeting Breaks, Incidentals $_____

Facilitator Time & Expenses $_____

Brochures (printing) $_____

Invitations & Response Cards (printing) $_____

Pre-Seminar Mailing $_____

Seminar Material Printing (packet) $_____

Follow-up (printing) $_____

Follow-up (mailing) $_____

Other _____ $_____

TOTAL: $_____

Biographies

Bob Currie -Senior Partner

Among all of Currie Management Consultants' worldwide staff, none understands manufacturers, dealers and their businesses better than Bob Currie.

He thinks likes his clients and understands their concerns because, as a business owner, he shares them. Bob founded Currie Management Consultants because — just like many entrepreneurs — he wanted independence, control over his work life and his future, and was willing to sacrifice to achieve these goals.

When combining this with his background, Bob is able to understand and serve his clients better than most corporate consultants ever could.

Bob began his consulting career over 30 years ago, first with a consulting group and then on his own, founding Currie Management Consultants in 1980.

Prior to that, he worked at Boston's State Street Bank in their mutual funds division, working on the fund now called The Vanguard Fund. After dramatically speeding up the fund's transaction execution speed, he consulted to other bank divisions, including Bank Americard, now known as Visa.

Bob prides himself on finding creative solutions to client problems. Whether it's in strategic planning, organization planning, finance, marketing, international management, market analysis, profit improvement, or dealership operations, Bob consistently takes a personal interest and an active role in his clients' success.

Besides solving CMC's clients' problems, Bob is always seeking new challenges to stretch and prove Currie Management Consultants' excellence, the latest of which is the consultancy's European expansion.

Whether it's challenging himself and his staff to excel, or challenging his clients to achieve, Bob Currie's passion and intensity drive everyone around him to greater success

Michelle Currie - Managing Partner

Michelle joined Currie Management Consultants in 1987 after a career as a magazine entrepreneur. She graduated from Regis College with a B.A. in management and earned her Master's Degree in Counseling Psychology from Assumption College. She also holds a certificate in cognitive behavioral therapy.

Michelle began as a management consultant, but in recent years her focus has shifted to a new area: business and personal development coaching.

After years of management consulting, Michelle saw that Currie Management Consultants' strengths in financial analysis, performance improvement, and project-specific consulting could be expanded and enhanced through consistent support and coaching of key staff.

Major goals and changes in company cultures can't be achieved unless the people who need to make those changes know what to change and how to change.

And after seeing that this human dimension wasn't always addressed, Michelle began offering personal and business development coaching to CMC's clients.

In her new role, she offers personal development coaching for executives and top level managers on issues including performance improvement, achieving goals, balancing work and life, both one on one and for groups.

Michelle has led workshops on topics such as customer relations, situational leadership, improving communications, assertiveness, and team building.

Prior to shifting her focus to coaching, Michelle worked in Currie Management Consultants' traditional areas, creating benchmark development programs, market analyses, pricing strategies, and management development programs.

Given her background, Michelle offers a unique mix of personal and business coaching services, helping clients to not only achieve their personal goals, but also improve management and business issues. So, just as she set out to do, Michelle and Currie Management Consultants can now create success in all aspects of their clients' lives.

George Keen - Partner

George focuses on operation, implementation and training for the construction, materials handling, and agricultural equipment industries at Currie Management Consultants.

He has conducted seminars on equipment sales and account management and consults on operational improvements and implementation, especially in service, parts, and rental departments.

He designs performance management, compensation, incentive, employee productivity, and company turnaround plans and works with dealer principals and service managers in dealer 20 groups (Best Practice Meetings).

George joined CMC in 1996 and was made partner in 2001. Prior to joining Currie Management Consultants, he spent eight years managing retail hardware stores and ten years at a company that developed software for the lift truck industry. George was a pioneer in the use of computers in accounting at a number of his early jobs, helping to move small business accounting and financial operations to computer systems in the 1960s and 1970s.

Continuing this trend of innovation, George spearheads CMC's e-learning and web conference program. George has led Internet training for companies in North America, Europe, and Latin America and has saved clients thousands of dollars and hundreds of hours of productivity by training far-flung staff simultaneously online. These training sessions have covered all aspects of dealership business, industry trends, and employee performance.

Matthew Hicks – Consultant

Matthew works with dealer groups in the lift truck, material handling, agricultural equipment, construction equipment, and power systems industries.

In this role, he coordinates and facilitates individual dealer projects, works on quarterly financial management meetings, company turnarounds, sales and account management work, dealership valuations, and other projects.

He joined Currie Management Consultants in 1999 after working in consumer credit for Toyota/Lexus. He earned his B.A. in General Business Administration from St. Michael's College in Vermont.

Matt enjoys spending time outside work with his son and wife. He also enjoys golf and is an avid sports fan.

Jeffrey R. LaBonte - Consultant

Jeff joined CMC in 1997 after graduating from Clark University with an MBA in Marketing.

Jeff has worked on a broad range of projects from business valuation, profit improvement, business succession and transition planning to benchmark development, distribution development and market analyses.

Jeff has also worked with CMC's Dealer 20 Groups in the industrial machinery, lift truck, compressor, construction equipment, agricultural equipment, transport refrigeration, and commercial tire industries.

Prior to joining Currie Management Consultants, Jeff worked at Bank Boston performing credit analysis and leasing work. He received his B.A. in Business Management from the University of Massachusetts Amherst.

Outside of CMC, Jeff spends his time with his wife, three children, and two dogs. Jeff is also an avid golfer and a private pilot.

Felix Vanholsbeeck – Partner (European Office)

The best consultant is one who deeply understands his clients' business. Felix Vanholsbeeck, the partner in charge of Currie Management Consultants' European operations, understands the industries he serves because he came to CMC from one of them.

Prior to joining CMC in 1998, Felix worked at Bandag, a global supplier of retread tires, where he was responsible for dealer management and development. Besides the years of management experience gained in that position, Felix was also a Currie Management Consultants client. While he was at Bandag, Felix and Bob Currie worked together to manage and implement a market expansion and repositioning program for Bandag.

Since 1998, Felix has managed CMC's Brussels-based European office where he manages local staff. The Brussels office provides the same range of services to clients as the U.S. office, but does so in multiple European languages including Dutch, French, English, Spanish, and Italian, and with a European sensibility.

In addition to his work at Bandag, Felix spent 12 years at Citibank, giving him a deep understanding and expertise in financial issues that he brings to each of his projects.

Felix graduated from the University of Brussels with the equivalent of three Bachelor's degrees, in Journalism, Germanic languages, and Commercial and Financial Sciences.

With a broad background ranging across such diverse subjects and in-depth experience in key practice areas, Felix provides innovative solutions and creates success for CMC's customers.

Additional Books
in the Profit Potential Series

Service Management Book

In today's marketplace it is often the case that the only differentiating item a dealership has is **Service!** Your service reputation can make or break a sales deal. Yet, most service training revolves around how to repair equipment and not how to increase service sales, improve customer satisfaction, and put money on the bottom line. Look at your financial statements and if you are not putting 25% or more of service sales to the bottom line you have something for you.

The Service Workbook: Achieving Profit Potential in the New Millennium is written using an easy to follow performance model that will drive service sales, customer satisfaction and profitability. This Workbook will take your service manager, service administrator, or the general manager step by step through the success factors for a service department.

This Workbook is now on the market for the low cost of $49.95. You are offering **The Service Workbook: Achieving Profit Potential in the New Millennium** direct to your dealership. Take advantage of this opportunity to purchase multiple copies – every service department, general manager, aftermarket manager, and controller will need a copy.

Consider what this book could do for your profits. If you found how to recover the $12,000 a year service vehicle expense for only one vehicle in your dealership, you would have made more than $11,000 on a $50 investment. Now, how many service vehicles do you operate?

Isn't this a good investment, then?

Short-Term Rental Management Book

Coming Next

Rental business is capable of being the second most profitable segment of the dealer/distributor's business – if run correctly.

The asset investment is large, so the focus must be on maximizing the revenue and maintaining the profitability. Many dealers find this a challenge.

CMC will illustrate alternatives that will help you manage a significant department in your organization.

Overview of a Successful Dealer

Handling Change Management

Currie Management Consultants will give you a glimpse of your potential and how to organize your company for better profits and productivity. Not only will you see the organization, but this book will include research from our work with over a thousand dealers who have used our methods and made significant change happen in their organization.

Order books on line at : www.curriemanagement.com